A Will Is Not Enough In Georgia

SIMPLE, PRACTICAL THINGS
A RESIDENT OF GEORGIA CAN DO TO

- ✦ PRESERVE ASSETS
- ✦ AVOID PROBATE
- ✦ AVOID GUARDIANSHIP
- ✦ PROVIDE FOR HEALTH CARE
- ✦ PROVIDE FOR THE FAMILY'S CARE

By AMELIA E. POHL, ESQ.
and
Georgia Attorney
CHARLES B. PYKE, JR.

EAGLE PUBLISHING COMPANY OF BOCA

D0684671

The purpose of this book is to provide the reader with an informative overview of the subject; but laws change frequently and are subject to different interpretations as courts rule on the meaning or effect of a law. This book is sold with the understanding that neither the authors, nor the editors, nor the publisher, nor the distributors of this book are engaging in, or rendering, legal, accounting, financial planning, or any other professional service. If you need legal, accounting, financial planning or any other expert advice, then you should seek the services of a licensed professional.

This book is intended for use by the consumer for his or her own benefit. If you use this book to counsel someone about the law or tax matters, then that may be considered to be an unauthorized and illegal practice.

WEB SITES: Web sites appear throughout the book. These Web sites are offered for the convenience of the reader only. Publication of these Web site addresses is not an endorsement by the authors, editors or publishers of this book.

EAGLE PUBLISHING COMPANY OF BOCA
4199 N. Dixie Highway, #2
Boca Raton, FL   33431   E-mail: info@eaglepublishing.com

Printed in the United States of America
ISBN 1-892407-79-5
Library of Congress Catalog Card Number 2002094574

A Will Is Not Enough In Georgia

CONTENTS

Introduction

Over the years, as we practiced law, we noticed that the questions people have about Wills, Trusts, powers of attorney, avoiding probate and guardianship, preserving assets, providing health care for themselves and their families, are much the same client to client. Many people are concerned about who will control their finances should they become too aged or too ill to do so themselves. Of even more concern is their health care:

Who will make my medical decisions if I can't do so myself?
How can I pay for my health care?
How much and what type of insurance should I have?
How can I avoid guardianship?

Others worry about the care of family members. Those with minor children worry:

Who will care for my minor child if I become incapacitated or die?

Is there a way to make sure my child has enough money to see him through college?

Those with elderly parents worry:

How can I manage my parent's finances should my parent become too aged or ill to do so?

Can my parent qualify for MEDICAID?

If my parent dies, will I need to go through Probate?

Is there a way to avoid Probate?

We agreed that a book answering such questions would be of service to the general public. We wish to thank all of the clients, whom we have had the honor and pleasure to serve, for providing us with the impetus to write this book.

Charles B. Pyke, Jr.

CHARLES B. PYKE, JR., a native of Atlanta, obtained a Bachelor of Science degree in finance at Auburn University. He went on to earn his Juris Doctor from the Emory University School of Law. Before Mr. Pyke founded Pyke & Associates, P.C., he spent five years as an associate at the Atlanta law firm of Ganbrell & Stolz. He also has work experience with the legal departments of various state and federal government agencies ranging from the Georgia Secretary of State to the United States Bankruptcy Court, Federal Home Loan Bank and the Federal Trade Commission.

As an attorney in private practice in Atlanta, Charles Pyke provides a wide range of estate planning services to his clients, with the primary focus on helping them provide security for their loved ones, reduce estate taxes, and avoid or at least minimize the costs and delays of administration, all with a well crafted estate plan. Mr. Pyke defines the mission statement for Pyke & Associates, P.C. as "Helping people be good stewards of all that has been entrusted to them."

Mr. Pyke is married and the father of two. He devotes much time to serving his community. Mr. Pyke is the chairman of the board of directors of the Southwest Christian Hospice and is on the advisory board at Christian City Home for Children. He currently attends Mc Donough Christian Church. When he can find time, Mr. Pyke enjoys horseback riding, hunting and water sports.

CHARLES B. PYKE, JR. is on the Board of Governors of the AMERICAN ACADEMY OF ESTATE PLANNING ATTORNEYS and regularly provides free educational seminars to the community on the subject of Estate Planning.

About the Academy

The American Academy of Estate Planning Attorneys is a member organization serving the needs of legal professionals concentrating on Estate Planning. Through the Academy's comprehensive training and educational programs on state-of-the-art Estate Planning law and techniques, it fosters excellence in Estate Planning among its members and helps them deliver the highest possible service to their clients. The Academy provides its members with excellent legal education, and top notch practice management support. In addition, each member is required to attain thirty-six units of continuing legal education annually.

The American Academy of Estate Planning Attorneys serves law firms in over 150 geographic areas in forty-four states. Clients who chose an attorney who is a member of the Academy can feel confident that they have an attorney who is dedicated to bringing them the highest quality of service.

The Academy is also committed to educating consumers on vital Estate Planning issues that touch their lives. Through its series of publications, educational programs and its consumer Web site, the Academy seeks to create a public armed with the information they need to become wise consumers of Estate Planning services.

 THE AMERICAN ACADEMY OF
ESTATE PLANNING ATTORNEYS
http://www.aaepa.com

Amelia E. Pohl, Esq.

Before becoming an attorney in 1985, AMELIA E. POHL taught mathematics on both the high school and college level. During her tenure as Associate Professor of Mathematics at Prince George's Community College in Maryland, she wrote several books including:
Probability: A Set Theory Approach,
Principals of Counting
Common Stock Sense.

During her practice of law Attorney Pohl observed that many people want to reduce the high cost of legal fees by performing or assisting with their own legal transactions.

Attorney Pohl found that, with a bit of guidance, people are able to perform many legal transactions for themselves. Attorney Pohl utilizes her background as teacher, author and attorney to provide that "bit of guidance" to the general public in the form of self-help legal books that she has written. Because there is such variation in the laws from state to state, each book written by Attorney Pohl is state specific.

With the assistance of an attorney licensed to practice in the given state, Amelia Pohl is currently "translating" this book for the remaining states.

Acknowledgment

We wish to thank Georgia attorney DANIEL D. MUNSTER for his editorial review of Chapter 10 of this book. In 1999, Mr. Munster founded DANIEL D. MUNSTER & ASSOCIATES, an elder law practice, focusing on Medicaid planning, advance directives (simple wills, Durable Power of Attorney for Health Care, Durable Financial Power of Attorney, and Living Wills), estate planning, and disability planning (special needs trusts).

Daniel D. Munster regularly teaches elder law to other attorneys, having previously presented on such topics as Medicaid, Medicaid Planning, advance directives, guardianship, and elder law litigation, before the Office of State Administrative Hearings. In addition, he regularly participates in community education programs presented at churches, senior centers, and assisted living facilities.

Mr. Munster has conducted Elder Law classes for the Evening at Emory program, appeared as guest attorney on *The Layman's Lawyer* television show, and has been featured on WGST radio. He has been published in various periodicals, including the *Georgia Bar Journal, Elder Law Today,* and *Lifestyle Transitions Magazine.*

Daniel D. Munster is a member of the State Bar of Georgia, the Atlanta Bar Association, the Atlanta Estate Planning Council, the Lawyers Club of Atlanta, and the National Academy of Elder Law Attorneys. He served as chair of the State Bar of Georgia YLD Elder Law Section, and on the Board of Directors of the Elder Law Sections of the Atlanta Bar and the State Bar of Georgia.

Mr. Munster maintains a Martindale Hubbell rating of AV, meaning that he is recognized for the highest levels of legal skill and integrity.

THE DESIGN ARTIST

LUBOSH CECH designed the cover of this book. He is a renowned artist, with extensive educational background and professional work experience. He studied design, applied art, and painting in his native Prague, Czech Republic. He also studied at the University of Bologna in Italy. Since moving to the United States in 1984, Mr. Cech has been designing art exhibitions, working as an art director, and graphic designer. Mr. Cech is a photographer and often incorporates his photographs into his art work.

Lubosh Cech is the founder of OKO DESIGN STUDIO located in Portland, Oregon. He designs promotional materials for print and digital media. He has received numerous rewards for both graphic design and painting. For more information about Mr. Cech and the OKO Design Studio visit his Web site.

http://www.okodesignstudio.com

The cover photo of Atlanta, Georgia was taken by Jeremy Woodhouse of Getty Images.

SPECIAL THANKS

We wish to thank Georgia attorney SUZANNE H. PRESLEY for her assistance in researching this book. It was through her help and encouragement that we were able to complete this book and get it to press.

Reading the Law

Where applicable, we identified the state statute or federal statute that is the basis of the discussion. We did this as a reference, and also to encourage the reader to look at the law as it is written. Prior to the Internet the only way you could look up the law was to physically take yourself to the local courthouse law library or the law section of a public library. Today all of the state and federal statutes are literally at your finger tips. They are just a mouse click away on the Internet. To look up a statute all you need is the address of the Web site and the identifying number of the statute.

FEDERAL STATUTES
http://www4.law.cornell.edu/uscode

GEORGIA STATUTES
http://www.legis.state.ga.us

Georgia has consolidated their laws into 53 numbered Titles. For example, Title 18 is Debtor and Creditor; Title 33 is Insurance; Title 53 is Wills, Trusts and Administration, and so on. Each Title is divided into Chapters and each Chapter is divided into Sections.

When referring to a statute we will give the number of the Title, chapter and section. For example (OCG 33-29-2) refers to: **THE OFFICIAL CODE OF GEORGIA**
TITLE 33, CHAPTER 29, SECTION 2
To look up the statute, you can go to the above Georgia legislative Web site. You can look up the code by typing 33-29-2 in the "Search" box.

If you come across a topic in the book you think is important, you may find it both interesting and profitable to read the law as it is actually written.

When You Need A Lawyer

The purpose of this book is to give the reader a basic understanding of Georgia law as it relates to Wills and other methods of Estate Planning. It is not intended as a substitute for legal counsel or any other kind of professional advice. If you have a legal question, you should seek the counsel of an attorney. When looking for an attorney, consider three things:

EXPERTISE, COST and PERSONALITY.

EXPERTISE

The State Bar of Georgia does not have a program to certify that an attorney is specialized in a particular area of law. This being the case, an attorney in Georgia may not represent to the public that he/she is certified by the state as a specialist in any given area of law. Attorneys are allowed to state that they concentrate on certain areas of law or that they limit their practice to an area of law.

There is a Lawyer Referral Service located in each county Bar Association. They will refer you to an attorney in your area who practices the type of law that you seek. You can reach the Lawyer Referral Service in your county by calling the State Bar of Georgia at (800) 334-6865.

One of the most reliable ways to find an attorney is through personal referral. Ask your friends, family or business acquaintances if they used an attorney for the field of law that you seek and whether they were pleased with the results. It is important to employ an attorney who is experienced in the area of law you seek. Your friend may have a wonderful Estate Planning attorney, but if you suffered an injury to your body, then you need an attorney experienced in Personal Injury.

Before employing an attorney, ask how long he has practiced that in that field of law and what percentage of his practice is devoted to that type of law.

COST
In addition to the attorney's experience, it is important to check what it will cost in attorney's fees. When you call for an appointment ask what the attorney will charge for the initial consultation and the approximate cost for the service you seek. Ask whether there will be additional costs such as filing fees, accounting fees, expert witness fees, etc.

If the least expensive attorney is out of your price range then you can call your local county Bar Association for the telephone number of the Legal Service office nearest you. The State Bar of Georgia has a Web site that lists Legal Service organizations for each county in Georgia,

 STATE BAR OF GEORGIA
http://www.gabar.org

PERSONALITY
Of equal importance to the attorney's experience and legal fees, is your relationship with the attorney. How easy was it to reach the attorney? Did you go through layers of receptionists and legal assistants before being allowed to speak to the attorney? Did the attorney promptly return your call? If you had difficulty reaching the attorney, then you can expect similar problems should you employ that attorney.

Did the attorney treat you with respect? Did the attorney treat you paternally with a "father knows best" attitude or did he treat you as an intelligent person with the ability to understand the options available to you and the ability to make your own decision based on the information provided to you?

Are you able to understand and easily communicate with the attorney? Is he speaking to you in plain English or is his explanation of the matter so full of legalese to be almost meaningless to you?

Do you find the attorney's personality to be pleasant or grating? Sometimes people rub each other the wrong way. It is like rubbing a cat the wrong way. Stroking a cat from head to tail is pleasing to the cat, but petting it in the opposite direction, no matter how well intended, causes friction. If the lawyer makes you feel annoyed or uncomfortable, then find another attorney.

It is worth the effort to take the time to interview as many attorneys as it takes to find one with the right expertise, fee schedule and personality for you.

The Organization of the Book

Many people who have a Will think they have their affairs in order, reasoning that should they die everything will go to the people named in the Will and somehow things will all be taken care of. But this is a simplistic view. There are many more things to consider.

1. What exactly will your beneficiaries inherit?
2. How will your property be transferred?
3. Can you (should you) avoid Probate?
4. Can you avoid a challenge to your Will?

The first four chapters of this book deal with these basic issues. Once you read these chapters you will have an understanding of what will happen to your property should you die, regardless of whether you do, or do not, have a Will.

The rest of the book deals with things a Will **cannot** do:

Chapter 5. Manage your personal debt

Chapter 6. Limit your business debt

Chapter 7. Provide care for a minor or disabled child

Chapter 8. Appoint someone to make your health care decisions should you be unable to do so

Chapter 9. Appoint someone to handle your finances should you be unable to do so

Chapter 10. Help you qualify for MEDICAID should the need arise

Chapter 11. Protect your home should you need to apply for MEDICAID

Chapter 12. Help your family settle your Estate.

A Will can't do these things but you will be able to do so once you read these chapters and understand what options are available to you under Georgia law.

GLOSSARY

This book is designed for the average reader. Legal terminology has been kept to a minimum. There is a glossary at the end of the book in case you come across a legal term that is not familiar to you.

FICTITIOUS NAMES AND EVENTS

The examples in this book are based loosely on actual events; however, all names are fictitious; and the events, as portrayed, are fictitious.

MALE GENDER USED

Rather than use he/she or himself/herself, for simplicity, we have used the male gender.

Your Financial Check-up   1

To understand why *A Will is Not Enough in Georgia* you need to know what a Will can and cannot do. One thing a Will can do is make a gift of all you own (your *Estate*). One of the things a Will cannot do is preserve and protect your property during your lifetime. For that, you need to think about risks to your property (poor investments, theft, loss through acts of nature, etc.) and what you can do to minimize or eliminate such risk. In other words, you need an *Estate Plan* for the care and management of your property during your lifetime.

The average person may protest "I don't have an Estate; none the less an Estate Plan." But you do. Everyone who has property, has an Estate Plan. You may never have verbalized your Estate Plan, or even thought about it, but it's there none-the-less. Take the case of the college student purchasing his first car. If his parents bankroll the purchase, the son may offer to hold the car jointly with them. The son's Estate is his car. His Estate Plan is to hold the car jointly with his parents so that they will own the car should anything happen to him.

This may not be the best Estate Plan. Holding the car jointly with his parents may make them liable for injuries or damages should the car be involved in an accident. If the young man's parents are familiar with Georgia law, they would be wise to refuse the offer and reassure their son "You can make a Will and make us the beneficiary of your car. But even if you die without a Will, we are your heirs under Georgia law. Either way we will inherit the car. Just make sure to drive carefully and carry enough car insurance."

1

This is a better Estate Plan. It gives the young man maximum control over his Estate (i.e., his car) during his lifetime. He can sell the car, mortgage it, or trash it, all as he sees fit. If he follows his parent's advice, of driving carefully and purchasing sufficient insurance, his Estate will have maximum protection. If he dies *intestate* (without a Will), and is single and without children, under Georgia's **Laws of Descent and Distribution**, his parents will inherit his Estate. And that is just the way the son wants things at this stage of his life.

Simple situation, simple Estate Plan. But, for most of us, life isn't all that simple. We may own many items of value and have loved ones who rely on us. At some point in our lives, we need to ask:

How can I make sure that my property will be inherited by my choice of beneficiary?

How can I arrange to have my property inherited quickly and at minimum cost?

How can I achieve these goals and yet have maximum control and protection of my property during my lifetime?

We will explore the different ways to answer these questions so that you can decide on an Estate Plan that is best for you. But before doing so you need to know what property you own; i.e., how much your Estate is worth. If you are married and your spouse handles all of the finances, it may be that you have no idea of the value of your Estate.

That was the case with Kristin. She met Matt when they were both at the pinnacle of their careers, but they had no more insight into their precarious position than fireworks in a summer sky just before self-destruct.

Kristin was a model. Not the best, nor the most beautiful, but she made a comfortable living. She moved in a circle of famous models. She reflected off of their radiance, making her appear more attractive than she actually was.

Matt worked in middle management for one of those high tech companies. Like Kristin, he was not particularly gifted but he happened to be in Silicon Valley just at the time the high stakes investors were showing extraordinary, if not misguided, confidence in the industry. The good times were rolling. It never crossed Matt's mind that this would one day end. He spent the money as fast as it came in.

Kristin was impressed with the lavish gifts Matt gave to her. She, and her family, thought she made quite a catch when she announced her engagement. After the wedding she continued to model, but it took a lot of traveling and Matt resented her time away. Eventually, she agreed to stop working altogether. After all, why should she, the wife of a wealthy man, need to continue with the rigors of a model's life of diet and exercise?

Matt never told Kristin about his financial difficulties. All she knew was that he was drinking quite a bit. Her suspicion that he also was into drugs was verified when he died, suddenly, because of an overdose. Her shock and sadness turned to anger when she discovered that all he owned was mortgaged and he was heavily in debt. He even borrowed money from her family without her knowledge!

Matt's creditors took it all. The house, the boat, the Porsche, everything. If only Kristin had investigated the true state of their finances, she could have arranged to set aside the money she earned prior to her marriage and not end up as she did, a destitute widow, past her prime.

DETERMINING YOUR NET WORTH

Even if you are single you may not know the value of your Estate because you have not taken the time to actually sit down and figure it out. To get maximum benefit from this book, you need to take a few minutes to determine your *Net Worth* i.e. the current value of your Estate.

ASSETS

$_____	Cash (certificates of deposit, bank accounts, etc.)
$_____	Tangible personal property (jewelry, motor vehicles, private art, stamp or coin collections, etc.)
$_____	Cash value of insurance policies
$_____	Securities (stocks, bonds, etc.)
$_____	Cash value of pension plans, IRAs, etc.
$_____	Cash value of a partnership or other business interest
$_____	Real property (residence, time share, lot, condo, cooperatives, etc.)
$_____	TOTAL VALUE OF ASSETS

It may be that you have a loan on your car or home, or any of the above items. You need to subtract away monies you owe to get the bottom line value of what you own:

LIABILITIES

$_____	Private loans
$_____	Mortgage Balance
$_____	Credit card debt
$_____	Car loan or car lease balance
$_____	TOTAL LIABILITIES

A simple subtraction gives you the value of your Estate.

ASSETS — LIABILITIES = NET WORTH

If you are married and hold all property jointly with your spouse, divide by 2 to get the value of your own Net Worth.

Your Net Worth is the value of all that you own, and that is how much your beneficiaries can inherit. Who will inherit your property depends on how your property is *titled* (held or owned).

There are three basic ways to title property:
⇨   in *your name only*   - or -
⇨   *jointly* with another - or -
⇨   *in trust for* another.

The way your property is titled determines who will inherit that property:

> Property held in your **name only** will be inherited by the beneficiaries named in your Will.
> If you have no Will, the property will go to your heirs according to Georgia's Laws of Descent.
>
> Property you hold **jointly** will go to the surviving joint owner(s) of that property.
>
> Property held in **Trust** will go to those you name as the beneficiary of the Trust.
>
> NOTE ⇨ If you are married, your spouse may have rights in your property, regardless of the way your property is titled.

We will examine each of these types of ownership in detail so that you can give yourself an Estate Planning check-up, i.e., you can check whether the way you are currently holding your property accomplishes your Estate Planning goals.

MINE, ALL MINE

There's much to be said about holding property in your name only and not jointly or in trust for another. There's maximum control. You can sell it, trade it, mortgage it, with no one to account to, or ask "may I?" How you protect your assets depends on how much security you require. Again, it's all up to you.

As discussed, there are three things to consider when setting up an Estate Plan:

CONTROL   How to control and protect your
             Estate during your lifetime.
BENEFICIARY How to be sure your Estate goes
             to the beneficiary of your choice.
COST   How to transfer your Estate to your
             beneficiaries at lowest cost.

Holding all of your property in your name only should give you maximum control and protection; but such an Estate Plan may present problems with the cost of transferring your property upon your death. More than likely it will take some sort of court procedure to transfer that property once you die. The name of the court procedure is *Probate*. In Georgia, Probate is conducted in the Probate Division of the County Court (OCG 15-9-30). We will refer to the court that handles Probate as the *Probate Court*. We will refer to property that is transferred to your beneficiary by means of a Probate procedure as your *Probate Estate*, and the person appointed by the Court to settle the Estate as your *Personal Representative*.

Probate can be expensive, so if you keep all of your property in your name only there could be a significant cost to transfer your property to the beneficiary of your Estate.

Holding property in your name should not create a problem with having your choice of beneficiary inherit your Estate, provided you have a valid Will. But if you die without a valid Will the Probate Court will use Georgia's Laws of Descent and Distribution to determine who gets your property. Of course it could be that the beneficiaries of your Estate under the Laws of Descent are exactly who you would have wanted, had you taken the time to prepare a Will. To help you determine if this is the case, we will take a few pages to explain the Law. Those who have a Will might be tempted to skip over the section, but, this information is good to know in the event someone in your family dies in Georgia without a Will. Once you read this section you will know whether you have a right to inherit his property.

THE FAMILY'S RIGHT TO INHERIT

The state of Georgia recognizes the right of the family to inherit property left by the **decedent** (the person who died); so the Laws of Intestate Succession cover all possible relationships beginning with the surviving spouse. In order for the spouse to inherit property under the Laws of Intestate Succession, the state of Georgia needs to recognize the union as a valid marriage.

Who Is Your Spouse?

In this era of people challenging the concept of the family unit, those of a philosophical bent may ponder the meaning of marriage. Is it a union of two people in the eyes of God? Is it even a union? Maybe it is just a contract between two people. The state of Georgia does not concern itself with such things. If a person dies without a Will, then the state will distribute the property according to the laws of Georgia; and the laws of Georgia determine whether two people are married.

BEING MARRIED IN GEORGIA

To be married in Georgia means that a man and a woman have obtained a license to marry from the state, solemnized the marriage by a state or religious ceremony, and then lived together as man and wife. A person must be of sound mind and at least 16 years of age to marry in Georgia. Parental consent to marry is required for anyone under 18. The age limits do not apply if the woman is pregnant or if both parties are the parents of a child born to them out of wedlock (OCG 19-3-2).

PROHIBITED UNIONS
Georgia law specifically prohibits the marriage of people:
- ☒ who are currently married;
- ☒ who are grandparent and grandchild;
- ☒ who are mother and son or mother and stepson;
- ☒ who are father and daughter or father and step-daughter;
- ☒ who are brother and sister. This includes siblings who are half blood; i.e. they have only one parent in common.
- ☒ who are aunt and nephew or uncle and niece.

Georgia law does not bar marriages between cousins (OCG 19-3-3).

THE COMMON LAW MARRIAGE
A Common Law marriage is one that has not been solemnized by ceremony. It is more than just living to-gether. The couple must agree to live together as man and wife, and then publicly hold themselves out as being married; i.e., tell friends and family that they are married.

Common Law marriages entered into within the state of Georgia before January 1, 1997, are recognized as being valid, provided they were at least 18 when they entered into the relationship and their union was not prohibited for any of the reasons given on the previous page.

Georgia will not recognize a Common Law marriage that was entered into within the state of Georgia after January 1, 1997 (OCG 19-3-1.1). However, Georgia respects the laws of other states, so even though Common law marriages are no longer valid in Georgia after that date, a Common Law marriage that is valid in the state where the couple entered into the marriage will probably be accepted as valid in Georgia, provided it is not a prohibited union as described on the prior page.

SAME SEX MARRIAGES
Vermont is the first, and so far the only, state to recognize a same sex marriage, which they refer to as a "civil union." California has laws which recognize *Domestic Partners* who are registered within the state. Hawaii has laws recognizing registered *Reciprocal Beneficiaries*. These relationships have the same rights and responsibilities of a married couple within the state. Several states (including Georgia) have passed statutes, specifically denying marital status to couples of the same gender. Georgia does not recognize a same sex marriage, even if that marriage is valid in another state or country (OCG 19-3-3.1).

The surviving partner of a marriage that is not recognized as being valid in the state of Georgia can inherit as a beneficiary of the deceased partner's Will, but the surviving partner cannot inherit as a spouse under Georgia's Laws of Descent and Distribution.

Now that you know whether the State of Georgia considers you to be married, the next question is whether the state recognizes anyone as your descendant.

Who Is Your Child?

Medical technology has made important contributions to solving the problem of infertility. There are all sorts of solutions, from hormone therapy, to sperm banks that provide donations anonymously, to frozen sperm or ova to be thawed and used at a later date, to women who become a surrogate or gestational mother. Solving a set of medical problems opened the door to a new set of legal problems.

Used to be, the only question was "Who's the father?" Now it could well be "Who's the mother?

To answer these questions, the State of Georgia has passed laws to legally establish the parentage of children whose conception was assisted by medical technology. We will examine the law as it relates to the right of the child to inherit property.

CHILD OF ARTIFICIAL INSEMINATION

Under Georgia law, a child born to a couple during their marriage, or within nine months of the time the marriage ended, is considered to be the couple's legitimate child. A child conceived by means of artificial insemination, is considered to be the child of the parents, provided both spouses have consented, in writing, to the use of the procedure. Regardless of who was the sperm donor, once the child is born, the husband is listed on the birth certificate as the child's father; and that child has all of the rights as any other natural child born of his parents (OCG 19-7-21).

A child born to a married couple using any other form of assisted conception has the same rights as a child conceived the old fashioned way. It is presumed that the husband consented to the assisted conception procedure. If that is not the case, and he is not the father of the child, he can *petition* (ask) the court to terminate his parental rights and responsibilities. If the husband is successful, the child will not be able to inherit from the husband, nor from his family.

FROZEN SPERM AND THE AFTERBORN CHILD

Under Georgia law a child conceived prior to death and born to the surviving spouse after the death, has the same right to inherit as any other natural child of the decedent (OCG 53-2-1). But suppose the child was conceived after death. Does that child have the same rights?

That question is becoming more of an issue as couples are freezing sperm, ovum or pre-embryo (fertilized cell) for use at a later date. Often the procedure is done to protect the cell from damage during cancer treatments. If the treatment is unsuccessful, the surviving parent may decide to go ahead with the pregnancy using the frozen reproductive cell. This raises issues of whether the surviving parent has the right to do that without the written consent of the deceased donor; and whether a child born of such procedure is entitled to inherit from the deceased donor.

This inheritance issue has important consequences, not only on the state level but on the federal level as well. A minor child who has lost a parent is entitled to Social Security benefits, but those benefits are based on the state's Laws of Intestate Succession; i.e., the state's Laws of Descent.

Section 216 of the Social Security Act provides "a child's insurance benefits can be paid to a child who could inherit under the State's intestate laws." Specifically, a child cannot receive Social Security benefits, unless the child is entitled to inherit under the state's Laws of Intestate Succession. This issue was brought before the Superior Court in New Jersey. The Court ruled that a child conceived and born after the death of a parent can inherit under New Jersey's Laws of Intestate Succession (*In Re Estate of Kolacy*, 322 N.J.Super. 593 (2000)). Other states have passed laws on the issue. For example, under Virginia law, the child may not inherit from the deceased donor, unless prior to death the decedent agreed, in writing, to the implantation.

Under Georgia law, a child born to the surviving spouse within 10 months of the death, who survives for at least 120 hours, has the same right to inherit from the deceased parent under Georgia's Laws of Descent as any other natural child of the decedent (OCG 53-2-1). As yet, the issue of the rights of a child conceived after the death of the donor/parent has not been raised in Georgia. However, because of this 10 month limit, a Court might rule that a child born after 10 months does not have the right to inherit from the deceased parent.

Those who decide to freeze their reproductive cells need to be aware of these issues. If you decide to freeze your reproductive cells, consider expressing, in writing, whether you want the cells to be used after your death. You may also want to state whether you intend that a child born of the reproductive cell be entitled to inherit your Estate. If you are married, it is important that your spouse join in the writing and agree to honor your wishes. If you freeze fertilized cells, your agreement should include instructions regarding what should be done with the cells in the event of a divorce or the death of either party.

Still another legal issue raised because of modern technology is the question of the rights of the Surrogate mother as opposed to the rights of the biological parent who contracted with the Surrogate to bear his/her child.

THE SURROGATE PARENTING CONTRACT

A Surrogate Parenting Contract is an agreement, usually between a married couple (the intended parents) and a woman (the gestational or Surrogate mother), in which the woman agrees to be the birth mother of a child conceived with the sperm of the husband, or the egg cell of the wife, or the embryo of the married couple, or none of these. This means that the husband or wife might be, but is not necessarily, the biological parent of the child born of the Surrogate mother.

Some states such as New York and Michigan consider Surrogate Parenting Contracts as being against public policy and have passed laws restricting their use. Other states, such as Florida and Virginia allow a couple to contract with a woman to have their baby, provided it is done according to the law of the state.

Currently there is no law in Georgia regulating the use of a Surrogate Parenting Contract. As it now stands, a child born to a Surrogate mother has the same rights as any other child born to the mother. If the Surrogate is married, and her husband agreed to the procedure, then he is the legal father of the child (OCG 19-7-21). After birth the Surrogate parents can agree to the adoption of the child by the intended parents. Adoption is necessary, regardless of whether either (or both) of the intended parents happen to be the genetic parent of the child. If the child is later adopted, the child will have the same status as any other adopted child.

THE ADOPTED CHILD

In Georgia, a person who is adopted has the same right to inherit property under the Laws of Descent and Distribution from his adoptive parents as does a natural child. This right extends to the adopted child regardless of whether the child was a minor or an adult at the time of the adoption.

The adopted child has no right to inherit from his natural parents under Georgia's Laws of Descent, with the exception of the natural parent who is married to the adoptive parent. For example, if a child loses a parent and is later adopted by a step-parent, the child has the right to inherit from his natural parents and from his adoptive parent as well (OCG 19-8-19, 19-8-21, 53-1-8).

THE NON-MARITAL CHILD

A child born out of wedlock has the same rights to inherit from his/her natural father as does one born in wedlock, provided any one of the following are true:

- ☑ The father married the mother after the child was born and acknowledged the child as his own
- ☑ The father signed a sworn statement saying that the child is his.
- ☑ The father signed the child's birth certificate.
- ☑ Paternity was established by a Court in this, or any other, state (OCG 19-7-20, 53-2-4).

If the decedent denied he is the child's father it will take a Court procedure to establish (or disprove) paternity.

Now that we know who the state of Georgia considers to be your spouse, and who is considered your child, we can determine how much of your Probate Estate each are entitled to inherit should you die without a Will in the state of Georgia.

GEORGIA'S LAWS OF DESCENT

Should you die with property titled in your name only, and without a Will, then the state of Georgia provides one for you in the form of the Laws of Descent and Distribution. Once your debts, funeral expenses, and the cost of the Probate procedure is paid, whatever is left (your *net Probate Estate*) is distributed as follows:

✧ **MARRIED, NO DESCENDANTS**
If you are married with no surviving **descendant** (child, grandchild, great-grandchild, etc.), then your net Probate Estate goes your surviving spouse.

✧ **SINGLE, WITH CHILDREN**
If you are not married but have children, all of whom survive you, then they will share equally in your net Probate Estate. If one or more of your children do not survive you, but your deceased child left surviving descendants, the descendants inherit the share intended for the deceased child **per stirpes**. Per stirpes is one of those legal terms that is best explained through example.

Suppose the decedent was unmarried with 4 children, Ann, Barry, Carl, and David. If he died intestate, and all his children survive him, then each gets 25% of his Estate.

CHILD WITHOUT DESCENDANTS DIES BEFORE DECEDENT
If Ann dies before her father leaving no descendants, then Barry, Carl and David divide the Estate between them. Each gets one third (OCG 53-2-1).

CHILD WITH DESCENDANTS DIES BEFORE DECEDENT
Suppose instead that only Carl and David survived their father. If Ann died leaving 2 children and Barry died leaving one child, then the Estate is divided into 4 shares — one for each surviving child and one share for each deceased child who left a descendant. Carl and David each get their 25% share. Ann's two children divide Ann's 25% equally between them (they each get 12 1/2%). Barry's child receives the share intended for Barry, namely 25% of the Estate.

✧ MARRIED, WITH DESCENDANTS

If you are married and have children, then they share equally in your Estate, provided that your surviving spouse gets at least one-third of your net Probate Estate. The children inherit your Estate in equal shares, per stirpes. For example, suppose you leave a spouse and three children, all of whom survive you. Your net Probate Estate is divide with one-third going to your spouse. The children share the remaining two-thirds (i.e., each gets approximately 22%).

✧ NO SPOUSE, NO DESCENDANT

If you have no spouse or descendant, your net Probate Estate is divided equally between your parents. If only one parent is alive, your Estate goes to that parent. If neither parent survives you, the Estate goes to your brothers and sisters in equal shares, per stirpes. There is no distinction between full blood siblings or half blood siblings. For example, if you have one brother with the same set of parents, and another brother with the same father and a different mother, each brother inherits an equal share (OCG 53-2-1).

If you are not survived by a siblings, but you have nieces and nephews, your net Probate Estate is divided between them, in equal shares, per stirpes. If there are no descendants of a sibling (nieces, nephews, great nieces, great nephews, etc.), your Probate Estate is inherited by any grandparent who survives you, in equal shares. If you have no surviving grandparent, your Estate goes to your aunts and uncles, in equal shares, per stirpes. If no aunt or uncle survives you, all of your first cousins share equally in your Estate (OCG 53-2-1).

THE STATE: HEIR OF LAST RESORT

If you die without a Will, with absolutely no next of kin, or if your leave a Will and no beneficiary can be found, then four years after the Personal Representative is appointed, he will ask the Probate Court to have the property turned over to the state of Georgia. If no one objects to the petition, the property is turned over to the county Board of Education and becomes part of the educational fund (OCG 53-2-50, 53-2-51).

THERE'S MORE TO THE LAW

The explanation of the Laws of Descent is abridged. We stopped the explanation at first cousin, but there is much more to the law. Even if you think you know who will inherit your property if you die without a Will, someone else may turn out to be the beneficiary of your Estate.

Why chance having your property go to someone you may not even know or like? Best to prepare a Will and have your property inherited by the person of your choice.

THE COST OF PROBATE

Holding property in your name only gives you maximum control and protection during your lifetime. If you do not like the way your property will be distributed should you die without a Will, then you can control who inherits your property by preparing a Will. But there is still the question of what it will cost to transfer your Estate to your beneficiaries. In all probability, a Probate procedure will be necessary. How much of your Estate will need to be spent to Probate your Estate?

Georgia is unique in that the heirs of a person who dies without a Will can ask the judge to allow them to transfer the decedent's property to the proper beneficiary without going through a formal Probate procedure.

NO ADMINISTRATION NECESSARY

In Georgia, your heirs can file a petition with the Probate Court asking the judge to issue an order stating that no administration is necessary. The request for No Administration is appropriate any time all of the following are true:

⇨ The decedent did not leave a valid Will.

⇨ No Personal Representative has been appointed.

⇨ All of the heirs who are entitled to inherit the decedent's property according to Georgia's Laws of Descent have consented to the petition.

⇨ The Guardian of any heir who is under 18, or disabled has consented to the petition.

⇨ There are no unpaid creditors of the Estate, or if there are, they have consented to the petition.

⇨ The heirs have agreed to the way the property (real or personal) is to be distributed (OCG 53-2-40).

If there are unpaid creditors who have not agreed to the petition, then they need to be notified of the petition. If a creditor is not notified, then once all of the property is transferred, each beneficiary is personally responsible to make good a valid debt against the decedent's Estate. The creditor has the right to sue each of the heirs individually, and all of the heirs together. If the creditor is successful, each heir is responsible to contribute to the payment up to the amount he inherited. But, if it comes down to a law suit, there will be attorney's fees in addition to the monies owed to the creditor. The heirs could end up paying more money than they inherited! (OCG 53-2-42).

On a positive note, if there are no creditor problems, your heirs can transfer all of your property to the proper beneficiary. The cost of making the transfer should be minimal.

THE FULL PROBATE PROCEDURE

A Full Probate Administration has more steps and takes longer than No Administration. It can be involved and time consuming — not to mention, expensive. The Full Probate procedure can take anywhere from several months to more than a year, depending on the size and complexity of the Estate. Once a Personal Representative is appointed he will take possession of your Probate Estate. Within six months of his appointment he must prepare an inventory of the Estate. Where necessary, he will employ an appraiser to evaluate the property (OCG 53-7-30).

Your Personal Representative must notify all of your creditors that they have a right to come forward and file a *claim* (i.e. a demand for payment) for monies that you may owe. Within 60 days of his appointment, he will publish notice to creditors to come forward and present their claims. He will have the notice published in a county newspaper, once a week for four consecutive weeks (OCG 53-7-41).

It is the responsibility of the Personal Representative to see that the Probate procedure is conducted properly. If the Personal Representative makes a mistake, then he may be responsible to pay for that mistake. For example, if he pays a debt that did not need to be paid — or if he transfers property to the beneficiaries too quickly and there were still taxes due on the Estate, then he may be responsible to pay for such error.

To avoid mistakes, the Personal Representative needs to employ an attorney to guide him through the process. It then becomes the attorney's job to see that the Estate is administered according to Georgia law and without any liability to the Personal Representative. The attorney for the Personal Representative is entitled to be paid a fee; and that fee is a proper charge to the Estate. There is no statutory guideline for what is considered as "reasonable" however, the attorney's fee is usually close in value to that paid to the Personal Representative.

THE PERSONAL REPRESENTATIVE'S FEE

The Personal Representative is entitled to a reasonable fee for administering the Estate. The amount can be specified in the decedent's Will or the beneficiaries can have a fee agreement with the Personal Representative. In the absence of fees set by the Will or by a separate written agreement with the beneficiaries, Georgia statute sets compensation as follows:

2 1/2% OF MONIES RECEIVED/PAID BY THE ESTATE

The Personal Representative is entitled to 2 1/2% of all monies received. This includes rental income, funds from a bank account, funds from securities that were sold, etc. This does not include Estate funds that he lent and that were later repaid. The Personal Representative is also entitled to 2 1/2% of the Estate funds that he used to pay debts or monies that he distributed to the beneficiaries of the Estate.

10% ON INTEREST EARNED

The Personal Representative is entitled to a commission of 10% of the interest earned on Estate monies he lent during the course of administration. He is also entitled to 10% of the annual income of real property that he manages as part of the Probate proceedings.

3% ON PROPERTY DISTRIBUTED

The Court can award up to 3% of the appraised value of the property distributed by the Personal Representative. The Court is not required to order an appraisal. The Court can determine the fair value of the property, and then base the amount of compensation on that value (OCG 53-6-60).

REASONABLE EXPENSES

The Personal Representation is entitled to be reimbursed for his expenses such as his traveling fees, and payment for people he employes such as appraisers, brokers, and his attorney (OCG 53-6-61).

EXTRA PAY FOR EXTRA WORK

The Personal Representative has the right to ask for more money than is allowed under statute 53-6-60, provided it takes more time and effort to settle the Estate than is usual (OCG 53-6-62).

The Personal Representative and attorney's fees are significant charges to the Probate Estate; but they are not the only charges against the Estate. A Probate proceeding can incur some or all of the following expenses:

$$ Court filing fees

$$ The cost of a bond that the Court may order for the protection of your Probate Estate

$$ The cost of notifying your creditors which may include publishing notice, or mailing notice to them by registered or certified mail

$$ The cost of an appraisal

$$ Accounting fees to prepare an inventory, and account for monies spent during Probate

$$ The cost of transferring property to the proper beneficiary; i.e., recording fees, broker fees to sell securities or real estate.

Once the above costs, Personal Representative fees, attorney fees, taxes and all valid claims are paid, the Personal Representative will distribute whatever is left to the proper beneficiary and then close the Estate.

You may be thinking that Probate is a good thing to avoid. Why should your Personal Representative go through all that effort to settle your Estate? Why should your beneficiaries wait months or maybe years, and pay all these fees to inherit your Estate?

There are ways to arrange your Estate so that your beneficiaries can immediately inherit your Estate without incurring unnecessary costs. In the next two chapters we will examine different methods that can be used to achieve this goal.

Is Probate Necessary? 2

Many people think that only wealthy people need to make plans to avoid Probate, yet each year, beneficiaries of relatively modest estates, spend thousands of dollars to settle an Estate. A bit of Estate Planning could have eliminated most, if not all, of the cost (and hassle) suffered by those families.

It is not difficult to arrange your finances to eliminate the need for Probate if you have a small Estate and only one or two beneficiaries. All you need do is title your property so that it automatically goes to your beneficiaries. There are many ways to arrange your finances to achieve this result. The most common method is to hold property jointly with another. Such an arrangement is the Estate Plan of choice for most married couples. Husband and wife often hold all of their property jointly, so that the surviving spouse has complete and immediate access to their property without any need for Probate.

Holding property jointly may not be the most desirable method for the single person, or for the surviving spouse who is now single. There are other ways to ensure that your property is inherited quickly and without cost to your heirs. In this chapter we explore the pros and cons of different methods of holding property so that it can be transferred without the need for Probate.

PROPERTY OWNED JOINTLY

Bank accounts, securities, motor vehicles, real property can all be owned by two or more people. If one of the owners dies, the survivor(s) continue to own their share of the property. Who owns the share belonging to the decedent depends on Georgia law and how ownership of the property was set up.

THE JOINT BANK ACCOUNT

When a bank account is opened in two or more names, the owners of the account sign an agreement with the bank stating who is to have access to the account during the lifetime of the account owners; i.e. whether each owner has full authority to make a withdrawal, or whether two signatures are required. The agreement should also state how the ownership of the account is to be transferred should one of the owners die.

Unless the agreement with the bank states differently, it is presumed there are *rights of survivorship*, i.e., upon the death of one account owner, the remaining joint owner(s) will own the account (OCG 7-1-813). A surviving owner is free to withdraw all of the monies from the account without the need to go through any Probate procedure to get that money, but understanding that he may be responsible to pay Estate Taxes on monies he inherits from the account (see Chapter 3).

You can arrange to have all of your bank accounts set up so that should you die, the money goes directly to a beneficiary, and without the need to go through a Probate procedure to get that money.

For example, suppose all you own is a bank account and you want whatever you have in this account to go to your child should you die, and without any responsibility to pay for your debts from that account. You might think that a simple solution is to make your child joint owner of the account, but first consider the problems associated with a joint account.

⊠ OVERREACHING

Making your child a joint owner of the account gives the child free access to the account. Monies may be withdrawn without your knowledge or authorization. You may be thinking that couldn't happen because you would immediately know of the withdrawal, and you could force the child to return the money. That may be true when you are healthy and alert. But in this ever aging society, it is likely that you will live to an advanced age and not be as aware as you are today. And if you have two children and decided to hold your account jointly with them, then there may be a problem with how the funds are distributed should you die.

That was the case with Amanda. All she had when her husband died, was a bank account worth $50,000. She wanted to be sure that the money would go to her two sons, Robert and Leon, without the need for Probate. She went to the bank with her two sons and opened a new survivorship account with all three names on the account as joint owners.

Several years passed without incident. As Amanda aged, her health began to fail, and she became more and more dependent on Robert.

She needed his assistance to take her to the doctor, to do her shopping, and of course take care of her finances. Robert had a wife and two children, so it was hard for him to care for his family and his mother as well. Leon was single, yet he never seemed to have the time to help care for his mother. And Robert resented that.

Finally, Amanda died.

After the funeral, Leon asked Robert about the bank account "Didn't Mom have a joint account in our names?"

"Yeah, but I closed it out. There was only a few thousand left, and I used it for her funeral."

Leon thought it strange that all of the money was gone, so he went to the bank and asked to see the record of withdrawals. He found that over the last two years Robert had written several large checks to himself. There was only $7,000 left in the account when Robert closed it out, within a week of her death.

Leon fumed for several weeks before he brought up the subject. Robert's face flushed when Leon asked about the money. Leon did not know if it was from anger or embarrassment. He soon learned that it was both when Robert asked "Where were you for the past two years? You never once helped. Did you know she became incontinent at the end? Who cleaned up? Not you. She blessed me every day. She often said she would have been dead long ago if it wasn't for me. She wanted me to have that money!"

"Mom never said anything to me about wanting you to have the money. She never asked for my help and neither did you. It isn't right for you to throw this up to me now."

The boys never spoke of the money again. But then there were few times that they ever spoke to each other after that.

Overreaching isn't the only problem with a joint account, there is also the problem of liability.

⊠   POTENTIAL LIABILITY
If you hold a bank account jointly with your adult child and that child is sued or gets a divorce, then the child may need to disclose his ownership of the joint account. In such a case, you may find yourself spending money to prove that the account was established for convenience only and that all of the money in that account really belongs to you.

Because of these inherent problems, you might want to hold the funds so that your beneficiary does not have access to the monies unless you die while the account is open. You can do so by opening a *Beneficiary Account*.

THE BENEFICIARY ACCOUNT

As explained, the terms of a bank account are established when a bank account is opened. Your agreement gives directions about who can access your account during your lifetime, but it can also give directions about what to do with the account should you die. If you hold the account in your name only and do not give any such directions, should you die while the account is open, the monies in your account will become part of your Probate Estate and will be distributed in the same way as any other item you hold in your name only.

One way to avoid Probate of the account, yet retain full control of the account during your lifetime, is to name one or more persons to be the beneficiary of your account.

There are two forms of beneficiary account. Your contract with the bank can direct the bank to hold your account *In Trust For* ("ITF") one or more beneficiaries that you name; or you can have a contract with the bank that directs the bank to *Pay On Death* ("POD") all of the money in the account to one or more beneficiaries that you name (OCG 7-1-810).

Under Georgia law, unless your contract with the bank says differently:

⇨ The beneficiary does not have access to the account during your lifetime.

⇨ You, as the owner of the account, have complete control over the account. You can add to it or close it or change beneficiaries without asking anyone's permission to do so (OCG 7-1-812).

If you are married, you may want to hold the account jointly with your spouse with directions to the bank to give the funds to one or more beneficiaries that you name. For example, ELDON CONNORS and LORRAINE CONNORS, JT TEN POD ELDON CONNORS, JR. AND FRED CONNORS

Unless the contract with the bank says differently:

⇨ During their lifetime, Eldon and Lorraine each own an equal share of the account, unless it is shown that each contributed a different amount.

⇨ The children (Eldon, Jr. and Fred) have no right to the account during the lifetime of their parents.

⇨ If either Eldon or Lorraine dies, the surviving party owns the account, and is free to close the account or change the beneficiary of the account.

⇨ Once Eldon and Lorraine are deceased, their sons share the money in the account equally. Should one son die before his parents, the surviving son will inherit the entire account (OCG 7-1-813).

THE TRANSFER ON DEATH SECURITY

The Georgia law for securities is similar to the statute for banks. You can instruct the holder of the security to Pay On Death or to *Transfer On Death ("TOD")* to a named beneficiary (OCG 53-5-65). As with the Pay On Death account, the Transfer On Death designation has no effect on the ownership of the security until the owner of the security dies. The security can be held jointly with another with instructions that once both owners of the security die, the security is to be transferred to a named beneficiary.

This is a convenient way of owning a security for the married couple who want a child to inherit the security without going through a Probate procedure. For example, a security can be held as follows:

TIM REILLY, OLIVIA REILLY, JT TEN TOD
STUART REILLY, LDPS

which is short-hand for:

TIM REILLY and OLIVIA REILLY own this security jointly. Upon the death of the surviving Joint Tenant, transfer this security to STUART REILLY. If STUART is deceased, transfer this security to his lineal descendants, per stirpes.

If your Estate consists of bank accounts and/or securities only, and you want all of your property to go to one or two beneficiaries without the need for Probate, but with maximum control and protection of your funds during your lifetime, then holding your property in any of these beneficiary forms: *In Trust For*
Pay On Death
Transfer On Death
should accomplish your goal.

REAL PROPERTY OWNED JOINTLY

If you own real property together with another, then who will own the property upon your death depends on how the current owner is identified on the face of the deed. The top paragraph of the deed should identify the person who transferred the property to you as the "Grantor." The person to whom the property was transferred is called the "Grantee." The deed might read something like:

THIS INDENTURE, made this day May 2, 2005
between ROBERT TRAYNOR, a single man,
herein called the "Grantor," and
SUSAN CODY, a married woman and
HENRY TRAYNOR, a married man,
JOINTLY WITH SURVIVORSHIP,
herein called the "Grantee," . . .
Grantor does hereby grant, bargain,
sell, alien, convey, transfer and confirm . . .
the real property with legal description

Robert Traynor is the *Grantor* of the deed. That means he transferred the property to Susan Cody and Henry Traynor who are the *Grantees* and present owners of the property. They own the property as *Joint Tenants*, meaning that should one of them die, the surviving joint tenant owns the property 100%. Nothing need be done to establish that ownership. Should the surviving owner want to transfer the property, all he/she need do is keep a certified copy of the death certificate to prove at closing that there is just one owner.

▤ DEED HELD AS TENANTS IN COMMON

You might have a deed that names you and another person as Grantee, followed by TENANTS IN COMMON. Should you die, your share of the property will go to whomever you named as beneficiary of that share in your Will. If you die without a Will, Georgia's Laws of Descent and Distribution determine who inherits the property.

If the deed names two or more people as the Grantee and does not say that they are "Joint Tenants" or "Joint Tenants and not as Tenants In Common" or "Joint Tenants With Survivorship" or "Jointly With Survivorship,"they hold title as Tenants in Common (OCG 44-6-190).

▤ DEED HELD AS HUSBAND AND WIFE

The indication on a deed that the Grantees are married does not mean that they automatically hold title with rights of survivorship. For example, if the Grantee on the deed is identified as a married couple, such as:

TODD AMES AND SUSAN AMES, his wife

without any reference in the deed to a Joint Tenancy or a Right of Survivorship, then the couple own the property as Tenants In Common.

A *Life Estate* interest in real property means that the person who owns the Life Estate has the right to live in that property until he/she dies. You can identify a Life Estate interest by examining the face of the deed. If somewhere on the face of the deed you see the phrase RESERVING A LIFE ESTATE, then the Grantee cannot take possession of the property until the owner of the Life Estate dies. For example, suppose a deed reads:

> This indenture, made this day, January 15, 2005, between ROSE MADDOX, a single woman, . . .
> herein called the Grantor,
> grants, bargains, sells . . .
> to SAM MADDOX, JR., a married man,
> herein called the Grantee . . .
>
> RESERVING A LIFE ESTATE TO ROSE MADDOX
> . . .

Rose is the owner of the Life Estate. Sam is the owner of the *Remainder Interest*. Rose has the right to occupy the premises during her lifetime or to rent it out and receive the income from the property. Sam has no right to the possession of, or the income from, the property, during Rose's lifetime. Once Rose dies, Sam will own the property and is free to take possession of the property and to lease, sell or transfer it, as he sees fit.

If you are an owner of the Life Estate interest, upon your death, no Probate procedure will be necessary to transfer the property to the owner of the Remainder Interest.

No Probate procedure will be necessary if you hold property in Georgia:

⇨   as the owner of a Life Estate - or -

⇨   as a Joint Tenant with Right of Survivorship.

In each of these cases, upon your death, the survivor will own the property 100%. If there is a Probate procedure for other property you own, then a title search at the time of transfer will reveal the fact that the survivor now owns the property. If no Probate procedure is necessary, all the surviving owner need do is keep a certified copy of the death certificate, and receipts showing that all applicable Estate Taxes have been paid. The surviving owner can present these items at closing should he decide to sell or transfer the property.

If you own real property in your name only, or as a Tenant in Common, some sort of Probate procedure will be necessary in order to transfer the parcel to the proper beneficiary. As explained in Chapter 1, if you die without a Will, your heirs can transfer property that you own in Georgia by having a Probate judge issue an order stating that administration is not necessary.

The procedure is called "NO ADMINISTRATION" but that is a misnomer because there are administrative things that need to be done. Your heirs still need to determine if there are any outstanding bills. The judge still needs to approve the transfer of the property to the proper beneficiary. Yet, No Administration is relatively simple. It can be done without appointing a Personal Representative and without the assistance of an attorney. You may decide not to have a Will so that your heirs can take advantage of the No Administration procedure.

This chapter relates only to property that you own in Georgia. If you own real property in another state or country, the laws of that state or country determine who has the right to inherit property in that state. Whether or not there are rights of survivorship depends on the laws of that state. In Georgia, property held as Joint Tenants means that there are Rights of Survivorship. But other states, such as Alabama, require that the deed specifically state that there are Rights Of Survivorship. In such states, a deed that identifies the Grantees as Joint Tenants, without saying there is a Right of Survivorship, is a Tenancy In Common.

It is also common practice in many states for a married couple to own property as *Tenants By The Entirety*. This is much the same as owning property as Joint Tenants. Should one partner die, the other owns the property without the need for Probate.

If you are married, and own property in your name only, you need to be aware that your spouse may have rights in that property. That is the case in Community property states. In other states, a surviving spouse may have Dower rights or other statutory rights. In the next chapter, we will discuss the statutory rights of a surviving spouse in real property located in Georgia. If you are married and own property in another state, you need to determine the rights of your spouse in that state as well.

Still another concern is whether a Probate procedure will be necessary to transfer out of state property that you own to your beneficiary.

Each state is in charge of the way real property located in that state is transferred. In most state laws, no Probate procedure is necessary to transfer the property to the surviving owner if the property is owned as Joint Tenants with Right of Survivorship or if the owner of a Life Estate dies. But if you own property in another state as a Tenant In Common or in your name only, a Probate procedure may be necessary in order to transfer the property to your beneficiary.

If you own property in your name only in this state and in another state as well, upon your death it may be necessary to have a Probate procedure in Georgia, and an *ancillary* (secondary) Probate procedure in the state where the property is located. This could have the effect of doubling the cost of Probate.

Still another problem with out of state property is the matter of taxes. Some states have an inheritance or transfer tax. Estate Taxes may be due in the state where the property is located as well as in Georgia. It may be necessary to file a tax return in two states. In addition to increased taxes, this can double the cost of the accounting fees.

If you own property in another state, it is important to consult with an attorney to learn the answers to all of these questions, namely:

Who will inherit my property under the laws of the state where it is located?

Will a Probate procedure be necessary to transfer that property to my beneficiaries?

Will a state inheritance tax need to be paid?

If you find that Probate will be necessary to transfer real property that you own in Georgia or elsewhere, you may decide that the cost of Probate is too expensive. You may be tempted to go for the quick fix of having the deed to the property changed so that you are joint owners with the intended beneficiary of the property; or you may decide to transfer the property to your intended beneficiary and keep a Life Estate for yourself.

This will avoid Probate, but it may not be the best Estate Plan because you will not have maximum control over the property during your lifetime. If you hold real property as a Joint Tenant or as a Life Tenant, you will not be able to sell that property during your lifetime without getting permission from your beneficiary. And if the beneficiary gives permission and the property is sold, the beneficiary will have the legal right to share in the proceeds of the sale.

You may be thinking "I can make my son joint owner of my home and avoid any need for Probate. I trust him to do what I want with the property. If I decide to sell, I know he won't ask for any part of the proceeds regardless of his legal right to those funds."

And all that may be true, but it may cost you more in taxes to sell your property than if you kept the property in your name only.

Under today's law, you can sell your home without paying a Capital Gains Tax, provided you lived there for 2 of the prior 5 years and the Capital Gains on the sale is not greater than $250,000 ($500,000 if married). If you sell your home after making the Life Estate transfer (or making your child a Joint Tenant), then unless your child occupies the home as his primary residence, his share of the property is subject to a Capital Gains Tax.

If your son does not take his share of the proceeds, then why should he pay any Capital Gains Tax?

In such case, you'll be the one to pay the tax on your son's share of the proceeds.

Is there a better way to avoid Probate?

Maybe. Read on.

How To Avoid Probate 3

TRUE OR FALSE?

( ) Probate is not necessary, if you die without a Will.

( ) If you have a Will, then Probate will be necessary.

( ) Probate is necessary if you own property that is worth more than one million dollars.

If you answered false to all of the above, you are either a lawyer, or you carefully read the last chapter. The first sentence is false because it could happen that there is a creditor problem and the judge refuses to grant an order of No Administration.

The second and third sentences are false because you may have arranged your Estate so that all of your property passes to your beneficiaries automatically, without the need for Probate, such as property held jointly. The point we were trying to make is.

> Whether Probate is necessary does not depend on whether you have a Will, or even how much money is involved. The determining factor is how the property is titled (owned).

There are three basic ways to title property:

- ✧ in your name only
- ✧ jointly with another
- ✧ in trust for another

Chapter 1 examined the pros and cons of holding property in your name only, with the biggest "con" being that Probate may be necessary.

In Chapter 2 we noted that holding property jointly with another solved the Probate problem, but at the sacrifice of the control and protection offered by keeping property in your name only. In this Chapter we examine another option which may be the solution to these problems, namely the REVOCABLE LIVING TRUST (also known as an *Inter Vivos Trust*).

A Revocable Living Trust is designed to care for your property during your lifetime and then to distribute your property once you die without the need for Probate. You may have been encouraged to set up such a Trust by your financial planner, attorney, or accountant. Even people of modest means are being encouraged to use a Trust as the basis of their Estate Plan. But Trusts also have their pros and cons. Before getting into that, let's first discuss what a Trust is and how it works.

To create a **Revocable Living Trust**, an attorney prepares a Trust Agreement in accordance with the client's needs and desires. The "Agreement" refers to the fact that the person setting up the Trust (the *Trustor* or *Settlor*) is contracting with someone to be the **Trustee** (manager) of property placed in the Trust. By signing the Trust Agreement, the Trustee agrees to manage the Trust property according to the directions given in the Trust Agreement. If the Trustor is the one who places property into the Trust, then he is referred to as the **Grantor**. The Trust Agreement also names a **Successor Trustee** who will take over the management of the Trust property should the Trustee resign, become incapacitated or die.

We will refer to the Revocable Living Trust as the "Living Trust" or just the "Trust" and the person setting up the Trust as the "Grantor." Usually the Grantor appoints himself as the initial Trustee so that he is in total control of property that he places into the Trust. In such case he signs the Trust Agreement as the Grantor and also as the Trustee who agrees to follow the terms of the Trust Agreement.

Once the Trust document is properly signed, the Grantor can transfer property into the Trust. The Grantor does this by changing the name on the account from his individual name to his name as Trustee. For example, if Elaine Richards sets up a Trust naming herself as Trustee, and she wants to put her bank account into the Trust, all she need do is instruct the bank to change the name on the account from Elaine Richards to:

ELAINE RICHARDS, TRUSTEE OF THE ELAINE RICHARDS
REVOCABLE LIVING TRUST
UNDER AGREEMENT DATED JULY 12, 2004.

If Elaine wants to put real property that she owns into the Trust, she can have her attorney or a title insurance company prepare and record a new deed with the owner of the property identified as:

ELAINE RICHARDS, TRUSTEE OF THE ELAINE RICHARDS REVOCABLE TRUST AGREEMENT DATED JULY 12, 2004.

The Trust Agreement states how property placed into the Trust is to be managed during Elaine's lifetime. Elaine, as Trustee, controls the Trust property. For example, monies she keeps in a Trust bank account can be withdrawn or added to in the same manner as if the account were in her name only.

Because the Trust is revocable, Elaine can cancel the Trust at any time and have the Trust property put back into her own name. If Elaine does not revoke the Trust during her lifetime, once she dies the Trust becomes irrevocable. Her Successor Trustee is required to follow the terms of the Trust Agreement as it is written. If the Trust says to give the Trust property to certain beneficiaries, the Successor Trustee will do so; and in most cases without any Probate procedure. If the Trust directs the Successor Trustee to continue to hold property in Trust and use the money to care for a member of Elaine's family, then it is the job of the Successor Trustee to use the money to care for the family member as directed in the Trust Agreement.

The Successor Trustee must also follow Georgia statutes relating to the administration of the Trust. For example, Georgia law requires that your Successor Trustee give an accounting to the beneficiaries at least once a year (OCG 53-12-190).

A Living Trust has many good features.

☆ AVOID PROBATE

As discussed in Chapter 1, Probate can be time consuming and expensive. Both the Personal Representative and his attorney are entitled to payment for their services. These fees can be significant. It may be necessary to hire accountants and appraisers, as well. If you have property in two states, two Probate procedures may be necessary (one in each state) and that could have the effect of doubling the cost of Probate. If the Trust is properly drafted and your property placed into the Trust, there should be no need for Probate. Upon your death, your Successor Trustee can transfer property, in this or any other state, to the beneficiary of your Trust.

☆ AVOID A CHALLENGE TO YOUR ESTATE PLAN

A Trust operates much like a Will because it provides for the distribution of your Estate when you die. Unlike a Will, it is not subject to Probate, so no Court is charged with the duty of "proving" that your Trust is valid. Your Successor Trustee can distribute your property as you direct, without asking anyone's permission to do so, and without giving the Court or any outside party an opportunity to examine the document. This does not mean that your Estate Plan cannot be challenged; but if the Trust is drafted according to Georgia law, and not with the intent of ripping off your creditors, or cutting off your spouse's right to inherit, it will be very difficult for anyone to challenge the document.

✰ PRIVACY

Your Trust is a private document. No one but your Successor Trustee and your beneficiaries need ever read it. If you have a Will, once it is admitted to Probate it becomes part of the Court records (OCG 50-18-70). Anyone can examine the Court records, read your Will, and see who you did (or did not) provide for in your Will. Other Probate documents such as the inventory of your Probate Estate, creditor's claims, etc. are also open to public scrutiny. In several states, Court records are now available on the Internet!

LEASE SAFE DEPOSIT BOX AS TRUSTEE

Another privacy issue is what happens to the contents of your safe deposit box, should you become disabled or die. Under Georgia law, if you hold a safe deposit box in your name only, then once the bank (or other safe deposit box lessor) learns of your death, access to the box is restricted. The bank will not allow anyone to look at the contents of your box without a Court order. In such event, any member of your family can petition the judge of the Probate Court for an order authorizing that person to examine the contents of your safe deposit box in the presence of an officer of the bank (OCG 7-1-356).

By leasing the safe deposit box in your capacity as Trustee, you can avoid having the bank officer (or anyone other than your Successor Trustee) examine the contents of your safe deposit box. You can instruct the bank that upon your death or disability, your Successor Trustee has full authority to enter the box and remove any and all of the items from that box.

☆ CARE FOR FAMILY MEMBER

You can make provision in your Trust to care for a minor child or family member after you die. If your family member is immature or a born spender, and you are concerned that he may spend, within months, what it took you a lifetime to earn, you can have your attorney prepare a Trust that will spread the inheritance over an extended period of time. Your Trust can direct the Trustee to give a certain amount of money every 5 or 10 years; for example, you can direct the Trustee to give part of the gift when the beneficiary reaches 25, another amount when he reaches 35, and then 45, etc.

You can set up a *Spendthrift Trust* for a beneficiary who is immature or a born spender. You can direct your Successor Trustee to use the Trust funds for the beneficiary's health care, education, and living expenses and nothing more. Georgia law allows limited protection for these monies. The funds are not protected from certain other debts, such as child support, or alimony owed by the beneficiary. They can also be used to pay for a judgment against the beneficiary for his wrongdoing; and they are available to pay taxes or other claims filed by the government against the beneficiary (OCG 53-12-28).

NO CREDITOR PROTECTION FOR GRANTOR

Although you can set up a Spendthrift Trust for the benefit of a family member, you cannot set one up for yourself. Property you place in your Revocable Living Trust is freely accessible to you. It is likewise accessible to your creditors both before and after your death. If you die owing money, your creditors can have a Personal Representative appointed to locate funds to pay those debts. The Personal Representative can require that your Trust property be used to pay for those debts.

☆☆ AVOID CONSERVATORSHIP

Once you have a Trust, you do not need to worry about who will take care of your property should you become disabled or too aged to handle your finances. The person you appointed as Successor Trustee will take over the care of the Trust property if you are unable to do so. If you do not have a Trust, and become incapacitated, a Court may need to appoint a Conservator to care for your property. The cost to establish and maintain the conservatorship is charged to you. As we will see in Chapter 9, such legal procedures can be expensive; and once established cannot be terminated unless you die or are restored to health (OCG 29-5-1, 29-5-72). With all these perks, you may be ready to call your attorney to make an appointment to set up a Trust, but before doing so there are a few things you need to consider.

THE CONS

⊠ COMPLEXITY

A Trust is a fairly complex document, often more than 20 pages long. It needs to be that long because you are establishing a vehicle for taking care of your property during your lifetime, as well as after your death. Your Trust may refer to 53-12-232 of the Georgia statutes and say that all of the powers stated are incorporated into your Trust. If such is the case, you need to read that statute so that you will understand all of the powers will be granted to your Successor Trustee.

Your Trust may be written in "legalese," so it may take you considerable time and effort to understand it. It is important to have your Trust document prepared by an attorney who has the patience to work with you until you fully understand each paragraph of the document and are satisfied that what it states is what you really want.

⊠ COST

Because of the thoroughness of the document and the fact that it is custom designed for you, a Trust will cost much more to draft than a simple Will. In addition to the initial cost of the Trust, it can be expensive to maintain the Trust should you become disabled or die. Your Successor Trustee has the right to charge for his duties as Trustee, as well as to charge for any specialized services performed. A financial institution can charge to serve as Successor Trustee, and also charge to manage the Trust portfolio. If you decide to have a financial institution serve as Trustee, then it is important that you compare the fee schedules of different institutions.

You can choose an attorney, or an accountant, or a financial planner, to serve as Trustee, but this may create a conflict of interest because the professional can use his position as Trustee to generate fees for himself or his firm. If you decide to appoint a professional as Trustee you should have a fee agreement stating what will be charged for his duties as Trustee and what will be charged for professional work done on behalf of the Trust. The fee agreement should be included in the Trust document with a provision that whoever accepts the job of Successor Trustee, agrees to accept the fee as provided in the Trust document.

You may decide to appoint your spouse or a family member as Successor Trustee, who may want little, or no, compensation. Regardless of who you choose to be Successor Trustee, you need come to a fee agreement. The agreement can be for a set amount or a percentage of the value of the Trust, or other method to be used to determine his compensation.

If you make no provision for fees in your Trust Agreement, your Successor Trustee is entitled to the same rate of compensation as a Conservator gets to manage a ward's Estate (OCG 53-12-173). As we will see in Chapter 9, that fee can be substantial.

⊠ ✫   THE TRUST IS LEGALLY ENFORCEABLE

Any beneficiary, or Trustee, of the Trust can petition the Probate Court or the Superior Court to settle a dispute arising out of the administration of the Trust. Georgia law requires the Trustee to keep the beneficiaries reasonably informed of the Trust assets and how the Trust is being administered. The Trustee must give the beneficiaries an annual accounting. If the Trustee is abusing his power or not accounting for Trust funds, the beneficiaries can ask the Court to have the Trustee removed (OCG 53-12-176, 53-12-190).

We gave this section a cross and a star, because the right to have a Trust enforced or administered by a Court is a double edged sword. It is great to have the Court protect the rights of your beneficiaries, but the cost of a Court battle could be greater than using Probate to transfer your Estate. Worse yet, your beneficiaries are at a disadvantage because the Trustee can charge the legal expenses to your Trust, while the beneficiaries must pay for their legal battles out of their own pocket. Even if the beneficiaries win the argument, the Trustee's legal fees are paid from the Trust, so there is just that much less for the beneficiaries to inherit.

⊠ ☆ YOU DO NOT NEED YOUR SPOUSE'S PERMISSION TO TRANSFER PROPERTY INTO YOUR TRUST

You do not need permission from your spouse to set up a Trust, nor do you need permission from your spouse to transfer property into that Trust. By putting all of your property into your Trust, you can, in effect, bar your spouse (or any other family member) from inheriting your property.

In many states, the law requires that a surviving spouse inherit a certain minimum value from the Estate of a deceased spouse. In some states, the surviving spouse has *Dower** or *Curtesy** rights. In other states, the spouse is entitled to a percentage of the Estate called an *Elective Share**. In Community Property states, the surviving spouse is entitled to half of the couple's *Community Property**.

A surviving spouse has no such rights in the state of Georgia. If the decedent did not provide for the surviving spouse, the most the surviving spouse can do is ask the Probate Court to require that a YEAR'S SUPPORT** be paid to the spouse from monies owned by the decedent spouse (OCG 53-4-1).

You may or may not think this is a good thing depending on whether you or your spouse is setting up the Trust, so we gave this section a star and a cross.

* See the Glossary for an explanation of these terms.
** Year's Support is explained on page 89.

⊠ PROBATE MIGHT STILL BE NECESSARY

The Trust only works for those items that you place in the Trust. If you own property in your name only, then upon your death, a Probate procedure might be necessary in order to transfer the property to your beneficiary. For example, if you purchase a security in your name only, without a "Transfer On Death" designation to a beneficiary or to your Trust, then a Probate procedure may be necessary to determine who should inherit the security.

The attorney who prepares the Trust usually creates a safety net for such situations. He prepares a Will for you to sign at the same time you sign the Trust. The Will makes your Trust the beneficiary of your Probate Estate. If you own anything in your name only, should a Probate procedure be necessary, the Will directs your Personal Representative to make that asset part of your Trust by transferring the asset to your Successor Trustee. Your Successor Trustee will add that asset to your Trust (OCG 53-12-71).

The Will prepared by the attorney is called a "Pour Over Will" because it is designed to "pour" any asset titled in your name only, into the Trust. Having the Will ensures that all of your property will go to the beneficiaries named in your Trust. But the downside of holding property in your name only is that a full Probate procedure may be necessary just to get that asset into your Trust. If avoiding Probate is your goal, holding property, in your name only, defeats that goal.

You can ensure that a Probate procedure will not be necessary by transferring your assets into your Trust during your lifetime, but if you neglect to put something into your Trust, the Pour Over Will stands by to transfer that asset into your Trust.

TAXES AND YOUR TRUST

Putting property into a Revocable Living Trust does not shield that property from taxes. All of the property held in a Revocable Living Trust is taxed as if the Grantor were holding that property in his own name. If the property earns income, income taxes will be due, and at the same rate as the Grantor would have paid if he had no Trust. Once the Grantor dies, both the federal and state government have the right to impose an *Estate Tax* on property transferred to a beneficiary as a result of the death. All the property owned as of the date of death becomes the decedent's *Taxable Estate.* This includes *real property* (residential lots, condominiums, etc.) and *personal property* (cars, life insurance policies, business interests, securities, IRA accounts, etc.). It includes property held in the decedent's name alone, as well as property that he held jointly or in Trust. It also includes gifts given by the decedent during his lifetime that exceeded $10,000 per person, per year. In the year 2002, the *Annual Gift Tax Exclusion* of $10,000 was increased to $11,000 to adjust for inflation (IRC 2503(b)).

For most of us, this is not a concern because no federal Estate Tax need be paid unless the decedent's Taxable Estate exceeds the federal *Estate Tax Exclusion* amount. That value is currently one and a half million dollars and is scheduled to go even higher.

YEAR	ESTATE TAX EXCLUSION AMOUNT
2005	$1,500,000
2006-2008	$2,000,000
2009	$3,500,000

Under current law, the federal Estate Tax is scheduled to be phased out in the year 2010, but reinstated once again in the year 2011 with an Exclusion Amount of $1,000,000 — unless lawmakers change the tax law once again.

THE GEORGIA "PICK-UP" TAX

The Georgia Estate tax is based on the federal Estate Tax. The federal government imposes a tax on all property transferred because of the death. The federal government then grants an Estate Tax credit, so that no tax need be paid unless the amount transferred is more than a given dollar value. We referred to that dollar value as the federal Estate Tax Exclusion amount. The Georgia Estate Tax is called a "pick-up" tax, because the state collects the tax that would have gone to the federal government had it not been for the federal Estate Tax credit (OCG 48-12-1).

As with the federal Estate Tax, no tax need be paid to the state of Georgia, unless the decedent's Taxable Estate exceeds the current federal Tax Exclusion amount. But for those Estates that are larger than the Exclusion value, Estate Taxes will need to be paid to the federal government and to the state of Georgia. And that includes property transferred within the state of Georgia regardless of whether the decedent was a resident of the state (OCG 48-12-3).

As explained, the federal Estate Tax is scheduled to be phased out and then reinstated in 2011. The Georgia Estate Tax is based on the federal Estate Tax credit, so unless the Georgia legislature changes things, the Georgia Estate Tax will go the way of the federal Estate Tax.

Both state and federal governments do not tax property passing to the decedent's spouse, however, once the surviving spouse dies, all of his/her Estate is subject to Estate Taxes. As explained on the next page, setting up a Revocable Living Trust can significantly reduce the amount of federal and Georgia Estate Taxes that may need to be paid once the surviving spouse dies.

A TRUST TO REDUCE ESTATE TAXES

Under current law, Estates of those who die in 2010 are exempt from federal Estate Taxes, but in 2011, the Estate Tax is scheduled to be reinstated and Estates worth more than $1,000,000 will once again be subject to a sizeable Estate Tax. A couple with an Estate in excess of a million dollars can reduce the risk of an Estate Tax by setting up his and her Trusts, so that each person can take advantage of his own Exclusion Amount.

For example, if a husband and wife own two million dollars, they can separate their funds into two Trusts each valued at one million dollars. The Trusts can be set up so that a surviving spouse can use the income from the deceased partner's Trust for living expenses. In this way, their standard of living need not be reduced by separating their funds into two Trusts.

If they do not wish to separate funds, they can set up a single Joint Trust that separates into two Trusts once one partner dies. Again, the surviving spouse is free to use the income from both Trusts. Once both partners are deceased, the beneficiaries of their respective Trusts will inherit the funds, hopefully with no Estate Tax due.

If the couple make no Trust provision, and they hold their property jointly, the last to die will own the two million dollars with only one Estate Tax Exclusion available. If lawmakers do not change the tax law, and the surviving spouse dies in 2011, or later, one million dollars of their Estate will be subject to an Estate Tax.

A Revocable Living Trust is a relatively simple way for a married couple to reduce, if not eliminate, the need to pay Estate Taxes; however, there is still the problem of the federal Gift Tax and the Capital Gains Tax.

THE UN-UNIFIED GIFT TAX

Up until the year 2002, if you gave someone more than $10,000 in any given year you had to report that gift to the IRS. As explained, the Annual Gift Tax Exclusion is now adjusted for the cost of living and is currently $11,000. The IRS keeps a running count of amounts you give to someone that exceed the Annual Gift Tax Exclusion. Although you are required to report amounts over the Annual Exclusion value, no tax is due unless that running total is more than the federal lifetime Gift Tax Exclusion amount. If your running total does not exceed that amount during your lifetime, once you die, the cumulative value of gifts reported to the IRS will be added to your Taxable Estate.

Up until the change in the tax law in 2001, the Gift and Estate Tax were unified. No Gift Tax needed to be paid unless the total value of the taxable gifts exceeded the federal Estate Tax Exclusion amount. That changed in 2004. In 2004, the federal Estate Tax Exclusion amount went up to $1,500,000, but the amount for the Gift Tax Exclusion remained at $1,000,000, so they are no longer unified.

To summarize:
If you make a gift to someone that is greater than the Annual Gift Tax Exclusion for that year, you must report the gift to the IRS. The IRS will keep count of values that you gave in excess of the Annual Gift Tax Exclusion. In 2004, and thereafter, if that sum exceeds $1,000,000, you will pay a federal Gift Tax on any amount you give that is over the Annual Gift Tax Exclusion. The Estate Tax is scheduled to be repealed in 2010, but not the Gift Tax.

The current federal Estate tax is scheduled to be phased out in the year 2010, but a new Capital Gains Tax is scheduled for 2010 that may prove even more costly than the Estate Tax. The new Capital Gains Tax is related to the way inherited property is evaluated by the federal government. Real and personal property is inherited at a "step-up" in basis, meaning that if the decedent's property has increased in value from the time he acquired it, the beneficiary will inherit the property at its fair market value as of the decedent's date of death. For example, if the decedent bought stock for $20,000 and it is worth $50,000 as of his date of death, the beneficiary will take a step-up in basis of $30,000; i.e. the beneficiary inherits the stock at the current $50,000 value. If the beneficiary sells the stock for $50,000, he pays no Capital Gains Tax. If the beneficiary holds onto the stock and later sells it for $60,000, the beneficiary will pay a Capital Gains Tax only on the $10,000 increase in value since the decedent's death.

Up to 2009, there is no limit to the amount a beneficiary can take as a step-up in basis. But in 2010 caps are set in place. The decedent's Estate will be allowed a 1.3 million dollar step-up in basis, plus another 3 million for property passing to the surviving spouse (IRS Code 1022(b)). The new law could result in significant Capital Gains taxes that the beneficiary must pay. For example, suppose in 2010 you inherit a business from your father that he purchased for $100,000 and it is now worth 2 million dollars. There is a capital gain of 1.9 million dollars, but you are allowed a step-up in basis of only 1.3 million. If you sell it for 2 million dollars $600,000 of your inheritance will be subject to a Capital Gains tax.

We will discuss methods of reducing the Gift Tax and the Capital Gains Tax in Chapter 7.

MAYBE A WILL IS BEST AFTER ALL

Although many methods can be used to transfer property without the need for Probate, it may be each method has a downside that is objectionable to you. Maybe you don't have enough money to warrant the cost of setting up the Trust at this time. Holding property jointly with another may raise issues of security and independence. Holding property so that it goes directly to a few beneficiaries in a Pay On Death account may not be as flexible as you wish. This may be the case if you want to give gifts to several charities or to a minor child.

For example, you can hold all your property so that it goes directly to your son without the need for Probate. If you ask him to use some of the money for your grandchild's education, it may be that your grandchild gets none of the money because your son is sued or falls upon hard times. If you keep your property in your name only and leave a Will giving a certain amount of money to your grandchild, the child will know exactly how much money you left and the purpose of that gift.

After taking into account all the pros and cons of avoiding Probate, you may well opt for a Will and a Probate procedure. If you make such a decision, it is important to keep in mind that Estate Planning is not an "all or nothing" choice. You can arrange your Estate so that certain items pass automatically to your intended beneficiary, and other items can be left in your name only, to be distributed as part of a Probate procedure. By arranging your finances in this manner, you can reduce the value of your Probate Estate, and that in turn should reduce the cost of Probate.

In the next chapter, we discuss the Will as an Estate Planning tool.

Those of you who have a Will may be thinking that there is no reason to read the Chapter, but does your Will:

- Make provision for the amount to be paid to your Personal Representative?

- Make gifts of your personal property? (jewelry, car, etc.)

- Name a Guardian to care for your minor child?

- Make adjustment for gifts or loans that you gave to the beneficiaries of your Will?

- Give specific instructions about how your bills and taxes are to be paid; i.e., which of your beneficiaries will have his inheritance reduced in order to pay your debts and taxes?

Has your Will been prepared so that it will be difficult for anyone to challenge it?

Have you stored your Will so that it is safe AND easily accessible to you during your lifetime and to your Personal Representative after your death?

If you answered "Yes" to all of the above questions, then you can skip over to Chapter 5.

Your Will – Your Way   4

Many people decide that the Will is the best route to go but do not act upon it, thinking it unnecessary to prepare a Will until they are very old and about to die. But according to reports published by the National Center for Health Statistics (a division of the U.S. Department of Health and Human Services) 2 of every 10 people who die in any given year are under the age of 60. Twenty percent may seem like a small number until it hits close to home as it did with a young couple.

Alex and Cathy were an old-fashioned couple in a modern world. When they married, they knew they wanted a large family. There was no question that Cathy would stay home and raise the children while Alex went to work. Luckily he did very well as one of the managers of a string of restaurants. Better yet, he enjoyed his work. He loved to cook and would even take over the kitchen when he returned from work. That suited Cathy just fine because she had her hands full raising their three boys.

Cathy couldn't help thinking how lucky they were that morning as she fixed breakfast. A nice house. Healthy, if not rambunctious, boys. All in all, a comfortable marriage. Her only concern that day was the fact that Alex was flying off on a business trip. All this terrorist news made her nervous about flying. Alex reassured her that it was only an hour's flight, and besides he was flying the company plane and not a commercial airliner.

But it was not terrorists that brought down the plane, just a malfunctioning rudder.

THINGS A WILL CAN DO

Though we all agree that one never knows, still people put off making a Will, figuring that if they die before getting around to it, Georgia law will take over and their property will be distributed in the manner that they would have wanted anyway. The problem with that logic is the complexity of Georgia's Laws of Descent. It isn't too difficult to figure out who will inherit your property, if you are survived by a spouse, child, parent or sibling. But if none of these survive you, the ultimate beneficiary of your property may not be the person you would have chosen, had you taken the time to do so.

Others think that it is not necessary to have a Will because they have arranged their finances so that all of their property will be inherited without the need for Probate. But money could come into your Estate after your death. This could happen in any number of ways from winning the lottery and dying (of happiness, no doubt) to receiving insurance funds after your death. For example, if you die in a house fire, the company that insures your home may need to pay for damages done to the property. In such case, the funds will need to be paid to your Estate. A Personal Representative may need to be appointed and the insurance funds distributed according to Georgia law.

If you die without a Will, your Estate may be distributed differently than you would have wished. And there are other important reasons to make a Will.

A Will Is Not Enough In Georgia

🗐 APPOINT A PERSONAL REPRESENTATIVE

The Court will give top priority to the person you name as *Executor* or Personal Representative of your Will. Without a Will, the Court will use the following order of priority to decide who will serve as your Personal Representative.

1st the surviving spouse unless an action for divorce or for separate maintenance was filed before the death
2nd an heir selected by a majority of the heirs
3rd any other eligible person
4th any creditor of the Estate
5th a person chosen by the Court to serve as County Administrator when no one else is appointed.

If two or more with the same priority want the job and cannot come to an agreement, then the Court will decide who should serve (OCG 53-6-20).

🗐 SET PERSONAL REPRESENTATIVE'S FEE

Once you decide on a Personal Representative, you need to check with that person to be sure that he is willing to serve in that capacity. And if so, then you should come to an understanding about how much compensation he will receive to settle your Estate. He is entitled to receive the amount stated under Georgia law, unless you make a different provision in your Will (OCG 53-6-60).

The statutory fee is substantial. At the very least the Personal Representative is entitled to 2.5% of value of the property he receives, and another 2.5% when he pays it out or distributes it to the beneficiaries. For example, an Estate worth $100,000 will pay at least $5,000 in commissions to the Personal Representative, and it could be significantly more (see page 21).

CAUTION

THE PERSONAL REPRESENTATIVE
CAN SEEK MORE MONEY

You can put the amount of agreed compensation in your Will; however your Personal Representative may decide to ask the Court for more money. To avoid the problem, you can have your attorney draft an Agreement that you and your Personal Representative sign and attach to your Will. With such a fee Agreement, the Court will not agree to the increase unless something unusual occurs (such as a law suit) causing much more work than with an ordinary Probate (OCG 53-6-60, 53-6-62).

You also need to keep in mind that the Personal Representative's fee is just to administer the Estate. It does not include payment for professional work he may do while settling the Estate. For example, if you appoint your attorney as Personal Representative, he can agree to the amount stated in the Will for his role as Personal Representative, and then ask the Court to award him attorney's fees as well.

The same goes for any other professional. If you appoint your accountant to serve as Personal Representative, he is entitled to receive compensation for his work as Personal Representative and also for any accounting work he does such as preparing and filing tax returns, preparing an inventory and doing an accounting for the beneficiaries. A financial planner who serves as Personal Representative may be compensated for his management of the Estate property (buying and selling securities, taking care of rental property, etc.) in addition to his fee to administer the Estate.

A Will Is Not Enough In Georgia

But the main problem with appointing a professional as your Personal Representative is the same as appointing a professional to serve as the Successor Trustee of your Trust; namely, that it creates a potential conflict of interest. The professional can use his position as Personal Representative to generate fees that might have been avoided had someone else settled the Estate.

When choosing a Personal Representative, consider the relationship of the Personal Representative to the beneficiaries and determine whether it would be better to appoint a non-professional for the job.

MAKE GIFTS OF YOUR PERSONAL PROPERTY

Another benefit to making a Will is that you can make provision for who will get your personal property (computers, antiques, securities, boats, snowmobiles etc.). When making a Will consider making provision for your car. If you make a *specific gift* i.e. a gift to a named beneficiary of your Will, it will be relatively simple for your Personal Representative to transfer the car to your beneficiary. If you do not make a specific gift of your car, your Personal Representative will decide what to do with it. He may decide to sell it and include the proceeds of the sale in the Estate funds to be distributed as part of the Probate Estate; or he can give the car to one beneficiary of your Estate as part of that beneficiary's share of the Estate.

SMALL GIFTS MATTER

Many who have lost someone close to them report that the distribution of small personal items caused the greatest conflict. If you arrange your finances so that no Probate procedure is necessary, your next of kin will need to decide among themselves how to distribute your *personal effects* (clothing, books, music collection, etc.).

Without guidance from you and no Personal Representative with authority to make decisions, there could be disagreement and hard feelings over items of little monetary value, but much sentimental value.

If you make a Will, you can include a list of gifts of personal effects in your Will and your Personal Representative will distribute those gifts according to your list. Of course, it is not possible to make a list of each and every item you own; but you can instruct your Personal Representative to allow certain family members to take their choice of items not mentioned in your Will. If two or more family members want the same item, instruct your Personal Representative to use an appropriate lottery system (coin toss, high card in a cut of a deck of cards, etc.) to decide who "wins."

 YOU CAN'T GIVE WHAT YOU DON'T HAVE

You need to give considerable thought whenever you make a specific gift to someone. It could be that you no longer own the item at the time of your death. This could happen with property or money. For example, suppose you leave all of your Estate to your son, with a specific gift of $10,000 to each of your three grandchildren. Your son is the **residuary beneficiary** of the Probate Estate, meaning he gets whatever is left once all of the bills are paid and all of the specific gifts made. If the cost of your last illness leaves your Probate Estate with only $30,000 to distribute, would you want the grandchildren to get their gifts and your son nothing? The simple solution is to make all of them residuary beneficiaries by leaving each a percent of your Estate. For example, instead of making a specific gift to each grandchild you could leave 70% to your son and 10% to each grandchild.

NON-PROBATE ASSETS

Property held in a Beneficiary Account, the proceeds of a life insurance policy, Trust property, Joint Property With Right of Survivorship and IRA accounts are all *Non-probate* assets because they will be inherited by your named beneficiary without the need for Probate. You cannot make a gift of such property in your Will because, you have, in effect, already made a gift of these assets. In fact, under Georgia law, the beneficiary of a Non-probate asset can only be changed by the owner of the property during his lifetime. The beneficiary of a Non-probate asset cannot be changed by Will (OCG 7-1-813).

📑 MAKE ADJUSTMENT FOR PRIOR GIFTS

You can make adjustments in your Will for gifts or loans given during your lifetime. For example, if you have loaned money to a family member and do not expect to be repaid, you can deduct the loan from that person's inheritance. There is no need to make the adjustment if the borrower gives you a promissory note because should you die, the monies will be owed to your Estate and the Personal Representative can deduct the monies owed from the borrower's inheritance. But if there is no evidence of the debt and you neglect to make a Will, the borrower will receive whatever is allowed under the Laws of Descent and Distribution (OCG 52-1-10).

Of course, it may be that you are not concerned with inequities. That was the case of an aged woman who had three children, Paul, Rita and Frank, her youngest. Frank always seemed to need some assistance from his mother. She often "loaned" him money that he never repaid.

Her other children were responsible and independent. Paul was married and had children of his own. He decided to purchase a house but was having trouble accumulating the down payment. His mother agreed to lend him the money. Paul and his wife offered to give his mother a mortgage on the property. The mother said a simple promissory note from Paul was sufficient, and she would have her attorney draft the note.

The attorney drafted the note but was concerned about the inequity "You never made a Will. Were you to die, each of your children will inherit an equal amount of money. If Paul still owes money on this promissory note, he will either need to pay the balance to your Estate, or have it subtracted from the amount he inherits. All of the money you gave to Frank will not count towards his inheritance unless you make your intentions clear that you considered the money you gave to Frank to be an advancement of his inheritance (OCG 52-1-10). You can do this by making an adjustment in a Will, or by having Frank give you a promissory note for any outstanding debts."

"It's O.K." replied the mother "I love all my children equally . . . some are a little more equal than others."

▤ MAKE PROVISION FOR PAYMENT OF DEBTS

Most Wills contain an instruction to the Personal Representative to ". . . pay all the expenses of my last illness, funeral expenses, costs of administration, taxes and just debts. . . " This does not present a problem if you are leaving all of your property to one person. That person will pay all of your bills and keep whatever is left. And there is no problem if you are leaving your Estate equally to several people because whatever is left will be distributed equally to those people. But if you leave a specific gift to someone and you owe money on that item, and do not indicate how the loan should be paid, that could create a major problem.

For example, suppose the mother discussed on the previous page, made a Will leaving everything to her three children, equally, with the exception of her car which she left to Frank. Further suppose, that she owed $10,000 on that car at the time of her death. If her Will did not specify that Frank was to be responsible to pay the monies owed on the car, he could demand that the Estate pay the debt. If his siblings refuse to pay the debt, the matter would need to be decided by the Court.

Considering how the mother treated Frank during her lifetime, it is probable that the Court will decide that it was her intent to have the $10,000 paid from the Probate Estate. Should the Court order the Estate to pay the loan, there will be $10,000 less to for the residuary beneficiaries of the Estate to inherit. That means that Paul and Rita's inheritance will be reduced to pay off the car loan, leaving Frank, as before, a little more "equal" than his siblings.

▤ MAKE PROVISION FOR PAYMENT OF TAXES

Taxes are another concern for those Estates large enough to be subject to Estate Taxes. State and federal law require that Estate taxes be paid by the beneficiaries of the Estate in proportion to the value received, unless the decedent made some other arrangements to pay for the taxes. If you make no provision for the payment of taxes, whoever inherits your property will pay a percentage of the taxes based on the amount they receive.

The beneficiary must pay his share regardless of whether he inherits the property through a Non-probate transfer (joint owner, beneficiary of your Trust, beneficiary of a Pay On Death account, beneficiary of a life insurance policy, etc.) or as the beneficiary of your Probate Estate. If a beneficiary refuses to contribute his share of the taxes, under federal law whoever is required to make payment (usually the surviving spouse or Personal Representative) can ask the Court to order the beneficiary to contribute his share of the taxes (26 U.S.C. 6324 (a)(2)).

If this is not as you wish you can direct your Personal Representative to pay all of your taxes from your Probate Estate. If you do so, beneficiaries of a specific gift, and those who inherit property from a Non-probate transfer will not contribute to the payment of your taxes. All of your taxes will be paid from your Probate Estate. This means that the amount that your residuary beneficiaries receive will be reduced by the amount of taxes paid.

CHOOSE A GUARDIAN FOR YOUR MINOR CHILD

If one parent dies, it is the right, and duty, of the surviving parent to care for the child. But it could happen that both parents become incapacitated or die before the child is grown. If you have a minor child, you can use your Will to appoint someone to serve as the Guardian of the child in the event that both you and the other parent are deceased (OCG 29-2-4).

You can even include a Trust in your Will, naming some-one to serve as Trustee to care for property that you leave to your minor child. See Chapter 7 for more information about how to make provision for the care of your minor child in the event of your incapacity, or death.

In Chapter 1 we explained that your beneficiaries could get possession of your property without a formal Probate procedure, providing you do not leave a Will. That may be just the way to go if you have a surviving spouse, no children, no creditor problems, and you want all of your property to go to your surviving spouse. But you will need a Will if you want your property distributed differently than Georgia's Laws of Descent, or you have creditor problems.

You may also want to have a Will for no reason other than putting someone (your Personal Representative) in charge of settling your affairs. Without a leader, getting your property, paying bills, filing taxes, and then distributing whatever is left, could be bedlam.

Regardless of whether you arrange for all of your property to pass directly without the need for Probate, it is important to have a Will for all of the reasons just stated. In Georgia, anyone who is at least 14 years of age, and who is not legally incapacitated may make a Will (OCG 53-4-10). A person is considered to have capacity to make a Will if he knows what property he has and makes a decision to distribute that property according to a rational plan that he has (OCG 53-4-11).

You may be thinking "That seems simple enough. I am certainly over 14. I know what I own and I know how I want to distribute it." But preparing a Will is like figure skating. It is harder than it looks. A Will needs to be clearly worded. A sentence that can be read in two different ways can lead to a dispute over what you intended; and that could lead to a long and expensive Court battle.

Your Will needs to be prepared according to Georgia law, and signed in the presence of at least two witnesses. Each witness must sign the Will, stating that you asked them be a witness and that they saw you sign the Will. Neither of your witnesses should be a beneficiary of your Will. If there are only two witnesses, and one of them is a beneficiary of your Will, then under Georgia law, the Will is still valid, but the beneficiary is not entitled to receive that gift (OCG 53-4-23).

The problem of having a beneficiary present when you sign your Will is one of **undue influence**. Undue influence occurs whenever someone exerts such pressure on the Will maker so that he is not acting according to his own free will (OCG 53-4-12).

If you are concerned that someone may challenge your Will, it is important that you consult with an attorney who is experienced in Estate Planning. The attorney will prepare the Will according to your wishes. If you meet with the attorney in the privacy of his office, and without anyone else present, it will be difficult to prove that someone was using undue influence to force you to make gifts according to their wishes and not yours.

Once the Will is prepared according to your direction, the attorney can supervise the signing of your Will. He will see to it that your Will is signed and witnessed in the presence of two disinterested witnesses — usually members of his staff. Each will sign the Will next to your name as witness; and they will sign a separate paragraph that says, they saw you sign the Will, and you did so of your own free will and at the time you signed it, you were competent to know what you were doing. Such a Will is considered to be *Self-proved* meaning that it can be admitted to Probate without any further testimony from the witness as to its authenticity (OCG 53-4-24).

Once signed in this manner it will be difficult for anyone to say that you did not know what you were doing when you signed the Will. If your Will is challenged your attorney will be able to present proof to the Court that the Will was prepared exactly as you wished, and that you had full capacity when you signed the Will. You can even have your attorney include a *no contest* provision in your Will stating that if a beneficiary named in your Will challenges your Will, he will inherit none of your Probate Estate.

Such a provision is called an *In Terrorem Clause* because it is designed to cause fear (if not terror) in the heart of your beneficiary. Many states will not enforce such a clause, because they want people to have the right to challenge a Will, and let the Court decide whether that challenge is proper. But Georgia law allows an In Terrorem Clause to be upheld, provided you make proper provision in your Will as to how your property is to be distributed in the event that a beneficiary challenges your Will (OCG 53-4-68).

This means that a statement such as "Anyone who challenges my Will gets nothing" may not be upheld, but a statement such as "I give $10,000 to John Smith, but if he challenges my Will, then I give this $10,000 to Mary Smith" can be upheld. If John is successful in his challenge to your Will, the Court will give the $10,000 to Mary.

STORING YOUR WILL

Once you sign your Will, you may wonder where to store it. If an attorney prepared your Will, he may suggest that he place it in his vault for safekeeping. By doing so, he ensures that your heirs will need to contact him as soon as you die. This does not mean that they are required to employ him should Probate be necessary. It only means that he will have an opportunity for future employment.

But there are problems with such an arrangement. The Will could be lost or mistaken for another Will. That happened in at least one case. The attorney prepared Wills for two people with the same name and similar family circumstances. When one person died the attorney submitted the wrong Will to Probate.

If you decide to allow your attorney to store the Will, you need assurance that the attorney will be responsible for the document. You should get a receipt and something in writing that says:

➪   The attorney accepts full responsibility for storage of the Will. Should it be lost or damaged, he will replace the document at no cost to you; and if you are deceased, he will, at no cost to your heirs, present sufficient evidence to the Court to accept a valid copy of the Will into Probate.

➪   There will be no charge to you, or your heirs, for the storage and retrieval of the document.

➪   Should he sell his practice, retire, or die, he or the successor to his practice, will return the original document to you.

THE SAFE DEPOSIT BOX, SAFE BUT . . .

You might consider placing your document in a safe deposit box that you lease at a bank. The only problem with the bank safe deposit box is convenient access. If you hold a safe deposit box in your name only, should you die, the bank will restrict access to the safe deposit box. They will not let anyone inspect the contents of the safe deposit box without a Court order.

Even with an order, the inspection will need to be supervised by an officer or employee of the bank (OCG 7-1-356). If your Will is there, they can forward it to the Probate Court. They will allow the person examining the contents of the box to remove any deed to a burial plot; and they will give a life insurance policy to the named beneficiary. Other than these items, the bank will not allow anything else to be removed without Court authority. Once a Personal Representative is appointed by the Court, he will have such authority. He will take possession of the contents of your safe deposit box. But if you arranged your finances to avoid Probate, it is self defeating to have entry to a safe deposit box trigger a Probate procedure.

For those who are married, the solution to the problem of accessing the safe deposit box after death, is to lease the box jointly with your spouse, such that each of you has free access to the box. As explained in Chapter 3, those who have a Trust can solve the problem by giving their Successor Trustee joint access to the safe deposit box. If you are single and do not have a Trust, you can lease the box jointly with a trusted family member.

Of course, if privacy and security are important to you, that may outweigh any concern you may have for the convenience of your beneficiaries.

STORE YOUR WILL WITH THE COURT

Residents of Georgia can store their Will with the office of the Probate judge in the county of their residence. This may be the best solution. The fee for doing so is nominal (currently $10). The Will is kept safe until it is needed. You are free to retrieve it from the Court in the event you move or decide to change your Will (OCG 15-9-37, 15-9-38).

Regardless of where you choose to store your Will, let your Personal Representative know that you have a Will and how to retrieve it in the event of your death.

I thought you said a Will is not enough

After reading this chapter, you may be thinking that the book is poorly named. After all, look at all the good things a Will can do:

* choose the person you want to settle your Estate
* arrange to have your Personal Representative settle your Estate for a reasonable fee
* give your personal items, including your car, to the person of your choice
* choose a Guardian for your child
* discourage a challenge to your Will.

But that is not all there is to an Estate Plan. A Will cares for your property when you are deceased, but it cannot provide for the care of your property in the event you become disabled. A complete Estate Plan provides for the care of your property during your lifetime and for the care of your person as well.

In these days of extended old age, many of us will need assistance with our health care and/or finances as we age. It is important to arrange to have someone manage finances and make medical decisions in the event that we are too aged or too ill to do so ourselves. These topics are covered in Chapters 8 and 9.

And a Will may be effective to transfer all that you own upon your death, but it cannot help your family pay for your debts. It may be that you have so many debts that your family is left with little or nothing. A complete Estate Plan provides for the financial well being of your family once you are deceased; and that is the topic of the next chapter.

Arranging To Pay Bills 5

You can think of your Estate Plan as being composed of two separate parts, a Lifetime Plan and an Inheritance Plan. Your Lifetime Plan provides for the care of your property during your lifetime, with the goal being maximum control and protection. Your Inheritance Plan provides for the inheritance of your property, with the goal being minimum cost and hassle to your beneficiaries. You could consider your Estate Plan to be a master plan that balances the goals of the Lifetime Plan with those of the Inheritance Plan.

When people consider their Inheritance Plan, they are mostly concerned about giving their possessions away. Many do not take into account how the bills they have accumulated will be paid once they are deceased, or even who will be responsible for paying those bills. Most of us do not worry about providing for the payment of our debts, thinking "I'll have that paid off long before I die." But with easily available credit, many are maintaining a high debt balance as a way of life. Paying off all of their loans is not a priority. Many will live their lives without ever being free of debt.

This does not imply that people do not know how to manage their funds. For many people (and corporations), it makes good sense to use other people's money to carry on business. In fact, great debt is a badge of honor for the wealthy. If a bank will lend you a million dollars, it means you have the means to repay that amount. Banks will not lend much money to those with few assets. Rich or poor, we all need to think about how our debts will be paid once we are gone.

Suppose you die without funds, and owing money. Does the debt die with you or is someone else responsible to pay what you owe? If you are married, the first person the creditor will look to, is your spouse. To understand the basis of this expectation, you need to know a bit of the history of our legal system.

Our laws are derived from the English Common Law. Under English Common law, a single woman had the right to own property in her own name and also the right to contract to buy or sell property. When a woman married, her legal identity merged with her spouse. She could not hold property free from her husband's claim or control. She could no longer enter into a contract without her husband's permission.

Once married, a woman became financially dependent on her husband. He, in turn, became legally responsible to provide his wife with basic necessities — food, clothing, shelter and medical services. If anyone provided basic necessities to his wife, then, regardless of whether the husband agreed to be responsible for the debt, he became obliged to pay for them. This law was called the DOCTRINE OF NECESSARIES.

In the United States, a series of Married Women's Rights Acts were passed giving a married woman the same right to contract, own property and run a business in the same manner as any single woman.

In Georgia, the property owned by one person prior to marriage remains his/her own separate property. Each party has the right to enter into his/her own contract. The non-contracting partner is not liable for the debt, unless the creditor can prove that there was fraud, and that the contracting party did not have the means, in his/her own right to pay for the item. For example, if one partner runs up a debt and then transfers all of his money to his spouse, the creditor has the right to seek payment from that spouse (OCG 19-3-9, 19-3-10).

Historically, Georgia Courts have ruled that a husband is liable to pay for the wife's necessities unless the wife purchased the necessities on her own credit, or under an agreement that she alone would be liable to pay the debt (*Citizens & Southern National Bank v. Parker*, 145 Ga. App. 802 (1978), 245 S.E.2d 48). But in these days of equal protection under the law, it is questionable whether this rule would be upheld should a husband challenge his duty for his wife's necessities when there is no duty for the wife to pay for her husband's necessities.

Paying for the necessities of a child is a different matter. Under Georgia law, both partners are equally liable to pay for food, clothing and shelter for their minor child. If one parent agrees to pay for the child's necessities, and does not have the means to pay for that debt, then the other must pay the debt. The only exception to this rule is that a parent who is divorced, and who has been ordered to pay child support, is not responsible to pay for necessities furnished to the child unless he agrees to be responsible for such payment in addition to his support payments (OCG 19-6-13, 19-6-14).

JOINT DEBTS

A *joint debt* is a debt that two or more people are responsible to pay. Usually the contract or promissory note reads that both parties agree to *joint and several* liability, meaning they both agree to pay the debt and each of them, individually, agrees to pay the debt. A joint debt can also be in the form of monies owed by one person with payment guaranteed by another person. If the person who owes the money does not pay, the *guarantor* (the person who guaranteed payment) is responsible to pay the debt.

A joint debt is payable from property owned jointly by the debtors. If there is no joint property, the creditor is free to seek payment from any of the debtors. If one of the debtors is deceased, the creditor can seek payment from his Probate Estate or from any of the surviving debtors (OCG 23-2-98).

Should you die, your hospital bills, nursing home bills, funeral expenses, legal fees for the Probate of your Estate are all debts of your Estate. They are not joint debts unless someone guaranteed payment for the monies owed. Hospital bills and nursing home bills can be considered to be necessities, so if you are married, the facility may seek payment from your surviving spouse. As explained, it is questionable whether they will able to collect payment from your surviving spouse, unless your spouse agreed to be jointly liable for the debt.

Your spouse is responsible to pay for loans signed by both of you. For example, if you both are authorized to use a credit card, and there is no money in your Estate, then your spouse must pay the debt. Property taxes are a joint debt if you and your spouse both own the property.

JOINT PROPERTY BUT NO JOINT DEBT

Suppose you have a credit card in your name only, and you have a bank account together with your son. Should you die, can the credit card company require that half of the monies in the account be used to pay the debt?

The answer to this question depends on how the joint property is titled. As explained in Chapter 2, there are different ways to hold property jointly with another. If the property is owned jointly with rights of survivorship, the surviving owner owns the property 100% as of the date of death. Georgia Courts have ruled the decedent's creditors cannot require the surviving owner to use property held jointly with rights of survivor to pay the decedent's debts (*Taylor v. Taylor*, 195 Ga. App. 711 (1990)).

BUT NOT EXEMPT FROM UNCLE SAM

Monies from a joint account with rights of survivorship go directly to the surviving joint owners. The funds are not part of the decedent's **Probate** Estate, but the decedent's share of the account is part of his **Taxable** Estate. If there are federal or state Estate Taxes due, whoever takes the decedent's share of the joint account, may be required to contribute whatever Estate Taxes are due on the decedent's share of that account.

NO RIGHTS OF SURVIVORSHIP

If the contract with the bank says that there are no rights of survivorship, or that the account is a Tenancy In Common, upon your death, your son will continue to own his share of the account. Your share of the account becomes part of your Probate Estate, and as such is available to pay your debts (OCG 7-1-813, 44-6-120).

PAYING FOR CREDIT CARD DEBT

Most of us are wise enough not to hold a credit card jointly with a child, but holding a credit card jointly with spouse is commonplace, especially if the card is being used to pay for necessities. If you hold a credit card with your spouse and you are concerned that it might be a struggle to pay it off should one of you die, consider purchasing credit card insurance to cover the debt.

Many credit card companies offer insurance policies and include the premium as part of the monthly payment. It benefits the credit card company to offer life insurance as part of the credit package, because they are assured of prompt payment should the borrower die.

Of course, in these days of high credit card interest rates, you might be struggling to pay your monthly credit charge. Adding still another charge to the account may not be an option, regardless of the security offered to your spouse. In such case, a better route might be for you to remove your name from the account and open a new account in your name only. This is especially important if you are using your credit card to pay for your business expenses, and not family necessities. Your surviving spouse is not responsible to pay for your business debts unless your spouse agreed to do so.

Still another reason not to hold a joint credit card is that each of you can establish your own line of credit in the event one of you retires or is out of work. Should the breadwinner of the family die, it may be difficult for the surviving spouse to establish credit if the spouse is retired and/or has no recent work record. It is easier for an unemployed spouse to establish a line of credit when he/she is married to someone
who is working.

OTHER TYPES OF LOAN INSURANCE

Many mortgage companies offer mortgage insurance to their borrowers. Mortgage rates are currently low, so an additional charge for mortgage insurance on the life of the primary wage earner may be worth the effort. This is particularly the case with families raising children. With such insurance, the family can inherit the homestead free of debt. The monthly insurance charge may be a small price to pay to ensure that the children can continue to live in their own home until they are grown.

Car loan insurance is still another thing to consider. If a married couple purchases (or leases) a car, and one of them dies, it may be a struggle for the other to pay off the loan. This was the case with Eva and Howard. Both had to work to support their three children. They owned two well used cars. It seemed that one car or the other was always in the shop. When they saw a *NO INTEREST* advertisement for a new car, they decided the offer was too good to pass up.

The monthly payments were high, but it was their only luxury. With both their salaries, they were able to make the payments. When Howard had his first heart attack, he was out of work for several weeks so they struggled to keep the payments current. Howard worked in construction, and was anxious to return to work. The doctors advised that such work might be too strenuous for his weakened heart. Construction work was all Howard knew, and the pay was good, so he ignored the warning and went back to his old job.

The second heart attack was fatal, leaving Eva as the sole means of support for her family.

With Howard gone there was no need for two cars. Eva could not afford the payments on the new car anyway, so she decided to sell it. Unfortunately, what she could get for the car was significantly less than the balance owed. Once she fell behind in payments she decided to surrender the car rather than have them repossess it. She was sure they would understand, considering all that she had been through these past several months, not to mention that she was a widow with three small children.

They didn't understand.

The company took the car and then sued for the balance of monies owed. The judge was sympathetic, but under the law there is no "life is tough" defense. He ruled that Eva had to pay the monies owed; and, as per the terms of the loan agreement, she even had to pay the fees for the company's attorney and all court costs. What an emotional and financial nightmare!

The pity was, it all could have been avoided, had they worked payment of debts into their Estate Plan. Howard was the primary driver of the new car and the primary wage earner. All he had to do was put the loan in his name only, and take out loan insurance. Eva would have inherited the car, debt free. She could have kept it or sold it as she saw fit.

Even if Howard didn't purchase loan insurance, had he put the loan in his name only, the company could only have sued his Estate. They would not have been able to sue Eva personally.

PURCHASING LIFE INSURANCE

The good part of purchasing loan insurance — be it credit card insurance, mortgage insurance or car insurance, is that you may be able to purchase the policy without taking a medical examination. The down side is that companies generally do not offer such insurance to those over the age of 65; and for those under 65 the cost of the insurance is a factor. It usually costs more to purchase loan insurance than a life insurance policy. Those in fairly good health need to comparison shop. If it is your goal to have insurance cover all of your outstanding debts, then the cost of a single life insurance policy may be much less than purchasing several loan insurance policies.

The Estate Planning strategy of purchasing life insurance to pay off all of your loans works best if you are married and your spouse is jointly liable for your debts. If you name your spouse as beneficiary of the life insurance policy, he/she can use the life insurance funds to pay off all monies owed. If you name your spouse (or anyone else) as beneficiary of your insurance policy, and that person has no legal obligation to pay your debts, then none of your creditors can ask your beneficiary to use the insurance funds to pay your debts.

The only exception is purchasing a policy to defraud your creditors. If a creditor can prove that you bought the policy to avoid using those funds to pay monies owed to him, a Court can order that whatever you paid for the policy, be paid to the creditor from the proceeds of the policy (OCG 33-25-11).

If you want the insurance funds used to pay your debts, you need to name your Estate as beneficiary of your policy. If you want someone to inherit money after you are gone, and you do not want those funds reduced by the cost of Probate or to pay off your debts, then naming that person as beneficiary of the insurance proceeds should accomplish your goal.

With or without debt, you may be wondering about life insurance — should you have it? How much is enough? The answer to these questions depends on the "sleep at night" factor, namely how much insurance do you need so that you won't worry about insurance coverage when you go to sleep at night? It is often more an emotional than a financial issue.

Some people have an "every man for himself" attitude and are content to have no life insurance at all. When they die, whatever they have, they have. And that is what their heirs will inherit. Others worry about how their loved ones will manage if they are not around to support them, and decide to purchase enough insurance to maintain their dependents in their accustomed life style. The same person may have different thoughts about insurance coverage as circumstances change — from no coverage in his bachelor days to more-than-enough coverage in his child rearing days to just-enough-to-bury-me in his senior years.

Insurance companies recognize that people's needs change over the years. Many companies offer flexible insurance coverage. As with any consumer item, it is a good idea to shop around. In addition to the problem of how much life insurance to carry, there is the concern of how the monies will be spent. Leaving a large sum of money to a person who is less than prudent, may lead to a spending spree.

ANNUITIES TO SPREAD THE INHERITANCE

Most beneficiaries go through their inheritance within two years. For many, the reason the money is gone so soon, is that there just wasn't much money to inherit in the first place. But for others, it's a spending frenzy. Luckily, people are fairly consistent in their spending habits, so you probably know in advance whether your intended beneficiary will "go wild," or prudently invest the monies he inherits.

If you want to leave an insurance policy benefit to someone you love, but the intended beneficiary is immature, or a born spendthrift, then a simple solution to the problem may be to purchase an *Annuity* rather than a life insurance policy with a single lump sum payment. You can purchase an Annuity from an insurance company so that upon your death (the *Annuitant*) receives money on a regular basis (monthly, quarterly, yearly) rather than one large payment.

Hopefully, this regular source of income will encourage your beneficiary to think ahead, and learn to budget his finances.

THINGS THAT CAN BE INHERITED DEBT FREE

There are certain items that can be inherited by your beneficiary free of the claims of your creditors. As discussed, your life insurance policy is creditor proof. And that is so, regardless of the value of the life insurance policy. There are other items that can be inherited free of debt under Georgia law:

✧ BENEFITS FROM A FRATERNAL BENEFIT SOCIETY ✧

Any benefit that is payable by a fraternal benefit society (e.g., AARP, American Legion, Kiwanis, Lighthouse for the Blind, Rotary Club, etc.) is free of the monies owed by the decedent. In fact, benefits paid by a fraternal benefit society are free from the claims of the creditors of the member of the society AND from the creditors of the beneficiary (OCG 33-15-62).

✧ WRONGFUL DEATH AWARD ✧

The surviving spouse has the right to bring a law suit if the decedent died because of the criminal or negligent act of a person or company. If there is no surviving spouse, the children have the right to sue. If the decedent is survived by spouse and children, monies recovered are divided equally between them, provided the surviving spouse receives at least one third of the recovery.

In the absence of a spouse or child, the Personal Representative can bring a law suit on behalf of the decedent's next of kin. Any money awarded because of the wrongful death is taken free of the debts of the decedent; i.e., none of the decedent's creditors can make any demand for payment from those funds (OCG 54-4-1, 51-4-2, 51-4-5).

✧ EXEMPTIONS FOR THE SURVIVING SPOUSE ✧
✧ YEAR'S SUPPORT

Under Georgia law, the decedent's spouse is entitled to receive a support allowance for at least a year following the death (provided she remains single during that time). The decedent's child who is under 18 and single is also entitled to a *Year's Support*, either as part of the spouse's allowance or a separate amount if the child is from a prior marriage. The spouse and child have a right to the Year's Support regardless of whether the decedent owed money or not.

The surviving spouse and/or Guardian of the child need to petition (ask) the Probate Court to award the Year's Support. The judge will set aside sufficient household furniture for the use of the spouse and will decide how much money or property must also be set aside for the Year's Support. The judge's decision will be based on the life style of the spouse and/or child prior to the death, and other income that is available to the spouse or child. Whatever the judge sets aside is free from the claims of the decedent's creditors (OCG 53-3-1, 53-3-3, 53-3-4, 53-3-7, 53-3-8).

DEBTOR'S EXEMPTION

Each resident of the state of Georgia is allowed to keep up to $5,000 in real or personal property free from creditor's claims (OCG 44-13-1). This statute does not state that this exemption continues once a person dies; but if the decedent was survived by a spouse, then the spouse can claim his/her own exemption for up to $5,000 of the personal property in the homestead.

BANKRUPTCY EXEMPTION

If you die without a Will and are survived by a widow or minor child and without enough money to pay all the money you owe, your surviving wife or child can inherit items that are exempt from bankruptcy in the state of Georgia, free of any creditor claim.

This includes:

⇨ Up to $20,000 in property that the decedent and his spouse owned as their **homestead** (principal residence). This includes ownership in a cooperative. The decedent's burial plot, or a plot he owned for his dependent can be included as part of this exemption.

⇨ Up to $3,500 in all motor vehicles

⇨ Up to $500 in personal jewelry used by the family

⇨ Up to $5,000 in household furnishings, clothing books, crops, animals, musical instruments, or household goods used by the family, provided any one one item does not exceed $300 in value

⇨ Up to $1,500 in professional books or tools used in the trade of the decedent or his dependent

⇨ Payment from an Individual Retirement Account i.e., an IRA account according to 26 U.S.C. 408, to the extent that the payment is reasonably necessary for the support of a dependent

⇨ A veteran's benefit, or Social Security benefit, or a disability or unemployment benefit

⇨ Any health aid that was professionally prescribed for the decedent or his dependent

A Will Is Not Enough In Georgia

⇨ A payment from a pension, annuity, or similar plan, to the extent that the payment is reasonably necessary for the support of a dependent.

The statute limits this creditor protection to the widow or child of a decedent who died without a Will. If there is a Will, the surviving spouse can still take his/her own $5,000 Debtor's Exemption. Georgia law does not allow a spouse to take both the Debtor's exemption and the Bankruptcy Exemption (OCG 44-13-43, 44-13-100).

NO EXEMPTION FOR PURCHASE MONEY CLAIMS OR TAXES
None of these items are exempt from monies owed on the item, nor are they exempt from taxes (OCG 44-13-107).

You may think the above title to be an oxymoron (a contradiction in terms). If a person is bankrupt, why plan for an Estate he doesn't have? But facts are, that people who file for bankruptcy are often quite wealthy and that is their downfall. Because they have substantial income or property, banks and people are willing to lend them money. If more money is borrowed than can be repaid, the unhappy result is bankruptcy. In the event you are concerned about meeting your responsibilities as parent or spouse, yet you enjoy a life style of financial brinksmanship, then consider investing in items that are "creditor proof."

That's exactly what Alan decided to do. Alan was astute, well aware of his strengths and weaknesses. He enjoyed his work and knew he had the capacity to earn large sums of money. But he also knew he was a gambler. Not the Las Vegas type, but a gambler in business ventures. "No risk, no gain" was one of his favorite sayings.

If you charted Alan's net worth over the years it would look like the peaks and valleys of the NASDAQ. Lots of high highs and low lows. Unfortunately, he married a woman who did not share his adventurous spirit. His wife became increasingly intolerant of their financial instability. She came to realize that this was his life style and things would never change. "All gamblers die broke," she said as she walked out the door with their 5 year old daughter in tow.

That, and the fact that he had to declare bankruptcy, brought Alan up short; and he began to be concerned about his future and that of his family.

Alan talked things over with his bankruptcy attorney "I am a good businessman, but not a clairvoyant. There was no way to predict the turn of events that led to this situation. But I know I will bounce back, and it will just be a matter of time before I earn my next fortune. I also know that I am an entrepreneur and not a 9 to 5 type guy so this could happen again. What concerns me is how to provide some security for my child in case something happens to me before she is grown." His attorney's response was a surprise: "Move to another state."

"You're kidding."

"Not really. There are few items in Georgia that are creditor proof. Many states have homestead creditor protection, so at least you can keep a roof over your head. A homestead in Texas or Florida is protected 100% even if it is worth a million dollars. Here in Georgia, only $5,000 of the equity you have in your homestead is protected from your creditors (OCG 44-13-1). Your creditors could force the sale of your home to pay for even a small amount of money that you owe. But you could put money into a federal retirement plan such as an IRA or Keogh account, and your daughter could inherit that free of your debts."

Alan didn't think that would work. "I am my own boss, and I don't have the self discipline to put money aside each month for my retirement."

The attorney explained "You can purchase a life insurance policy with your wife or daughter as beneficiary. Regardless of the value of the policy, they would inherit the proceeds free of your debts. The only problem with an insurance policy, is that the cash value of the policy is available to your creditors during your lifetime.

Alan was annoyed "You're saying that here in Georgia, while I am alive, I can protect $5,000 of the equity in my home and my retirement funds? What about all those millionaires who protect their money in Offshore Trusts? If I really hit it big, why can't I do that?"

"You could, but there are many drawbacks. Just to set up an offshore Trust costs tens of thousands of dollars, not to mention how much it would cost just to maintain the Trust."

Alan said "Yes, but if I had millions of dollars that would not be a problem."

"True, but there are other considerations. Once you put your money into the Trust, you are essentially giving up control of that money."

Alan was skeptical "Oh come now. Why would anyone put his money where he can't get to it?"

The attorney explained "The Trust can be set up so that funds are available for whatever the millionaire wants. Usually funds are made available to support his family. Trust funds can be used to maintain the family home or yacht. Monies from the Trust can be used to pay for travel or for an expensive vacation. And of course the Trust would provide for the transfer of the property to the millionaire's beneficiaries, once the millionaire dies. What the millionaire can't do is be the Trustee of the Trust, because if he were, he would have control over the money, and his creditors could take legal action here in the United States to force him to use his Trustee powers to use that money to pay his creditors."

"How can they force the issue? Why couldn't he, as Trustee, just refuse?"

"Remember, that as long as the millionaire is a citizen of the United States, and he is physically present in the states, he is subject to the laws of this country. If a creditor goes to Court and wins, the U. S. judge could order the millionaire, as Trustee, to use Trust funds to pay that debt. If the millionaire-Trustee refused, the judge could put him in jail for contempt of Court. No, for an Offshore Trust to work, the Trust must be a foreign Trust, that is, drafted according to the laws of a foreign country, Trust property must be located outside of the United States, and the Trustee cannot be a citizen of the United States."

Alan said "Well I guess the millionaire might have a relative who is not a U.S. citizen to manage the Trust."

The attorney agreed "Yes, or he could use a financial institution that does not do business in the U.S., to manage the funds. But there are other problems with an Offshore Trust. There's the safety factor. Trust funds are kept outside of the United States. If the funds are kept in a foreign bank and the country suffers an economic collapse, then those funds could be lost."

Alan wondered "Isn't that much the same risk as money in a U.S. bank? Only $100,000 of the cash in a U. S. bank account is insured. If the bank fails, any money in that bank over $100,000 could be lost."

The attorney disagreed "Our U.S government is stable, and we trust that they will regulate U.S. banks and keep our money safe. But that is not the case with other small countries. The government of a small country could collapse and the banks along with it."

"But why keep money in a bank? Most millionaires have their funds invested in stocks and bonds, or in real property."

The attorney agreed "True, but real estate could be risky. If your Trust contains real property located within the United States, your creditor could go to a U.S. court and take that property."

Alan wondered "Couldn't the creditor take the overseas property as well?"

"He could, but it would be hard. For one thing he would need to find the property. And the Trustee is not about to tell him where it is, unless the creditor sues, and the laws of that foreign country require the Trustee to tell. Even if the creditor locates Trust property, whether it is stocks, bonds, or real estate, most Offshore Trusts are established in countries that are not creditor friendly. For example, if you set up an off shore Trust in the Cook Islands, they will not accept a judgment that a creditor got in the United States. The creditor will need to employ a Cook Islands attorney to sue you all over again in the Cook Islands. That's expensive. And the Cook Islands have a higher standard of proof. Here in the U.S., all your creditor need do is to show that you owe the money *by a preponderance of the evidence.* That's lawyer talk for "the jury must be more than 50% sure you owe the money." In the Cook Islands, the creditor's attorney must prove you owe the money *beyond a reasonable doubt* (Cook Islands, International Trusts Act of 1984 Section 13B(1)). That standard is the one we use here in the U.S. for criminal cases. In addition, the foreign country usually has a short Statute of Limitations, so if your creditor does not sue you in that country within that period of time, he cannot sue you at all."

Alan said "I can see why Offshore Trusts are so popular."

The attorney cautioned "But there are other problems. The U.S. considers transfers into and/or out of the Trust to be taxable. The IRS requires special tax returns to be filed for all foreign Trusts. In addition, the IRS looks closely at Offshore Trusts to determine whether they are fraudulent transfers, designed to avoid U.S. income taxes or U.S. Estate taxes. The IRS wants to be sure that the creditor the millionaire is avoiding isn't Uncle Sam!"

Alan said "Yes, but if you pay your taxes, that shouldn't be a problem. If I ever get to the point where I am that wealthy, I'll come back to discuss setting up an Offshore Trust."

The attorney refused "No, I'm just a country lawyer. If you want to go that route, you need a specialist — someone who has overseas connections, and who has experience in writing such Trusts. If you are serious about setting up an Offshore Trust, let me know and I will recommend someone to you."

"O.K. I will."

The attorney offered a final word of caution "If you are able to accumulate a significant amount of money, don't risk it all in a business venture. Limit the amount of money you can lose to just the money that you invest in business. Keep your personal funds separate and protected from your business debts. If you want to start a business, make sure that you cannot be personally liable for your business debts. You can avoid personal liability by forming a corporation, or a Limited Partnership, or a Limited Liability Company.** Stay away from a sole proprietorship or a business partnership."

** These topics are discussed in the next chapter.

Your Business Estate Plan 6

It would take a very thick book to do justice to the topic of Business Estate Planning. Estate Planning issues must be discussed for each type of business:

CONTROL   How to control and protect your
             business during your lifetime.

BENEFICIARY How to be sure your business goes
             to the beneficiary of your choice.

COST   How to transfer your business to your
             beneficiary quickly and at lowest cost.

With just one chapter to devote to the topic, we can only provide the reader with an overview of the subject. Hopefully, the overview will give the reader some ideas that can later be pursued with a financial planner, or an attorney.

We have written this chapter for the reader who listed a business value as part of his Net Worth on page 4. People who are self employed, but who do not think of themselves as business owners, may profit from the information covered in this chapter, as well.

This chapter should also be of interest to someone who has the possibility of inheriting a business interest, such as the child of a small business owner, or perhaps the spouse of someone who is self employed. Even those who are thinking of starting a business, may find it worthwhile to take a few minutes to read this chapter.

Those who have no present business interest may want to skip this chapter and go on to Chapter 7.

Your business is your property, and as such it is included as part of your overall Estate Plan. But owning a business isn't as simple as just holding title to property such as a car or parcel of real estate. For example, if you own a business in your name only, i.e. as a *sole proprietor*, there may be no single document that indicates ownership of your business property. If you are doing business under a trade name, you probably filed a Registration Statement with the Clerk of the Superior Court in the county where you are conducting business (OCG 10-1-490).

The Clerk keeps an alphabetical index of Registration Statements filed with his office. The Registration Statement identifies the trade name of the business and the name and address of the owner of the business; but it does not identify business property. You could have a truck, computers, copiers or other expensive business equipment. Title to that business property is probably in your own personal name.

Your business bank account may be in your name only, or in the trade name of the business with you alone as signatory on the account. Charge cards and business loans are either in your name only, or in the trade name with your name as guarantor.

If you want to leave your business to your son, how do you do it? Do you leave him the equipment used in the business? If you are doing business under your own name and not a registered trade name, how do you give him that name? And how do you handle business related loans? If you leave him the business, will he agree to be responsible for any outstanding business debt?

Partnerships can be even more complicated, unless there is a written partnership agreement that says how the business is to be transferred in the event that one of the partners dies. Even the transfer of a corporation can be a major headache if there are several shareholders and no shareholders' agreement to say how shares should be transferred in the event of the death or incapacity of the shareholder.

For these reasons, it is important to think about an Estate Plan for your business. You need to ask yourself:

> *How can I have maximum protection and control over my business during my lifetime?*
>
> *How can I structure my business so that it can be transferred quickly and at minimum cost?*

We will examine each type of business ownership as it relates to the these questions.

WHAT'S THE BEST TYPE OF BUSINESS OWNERSHIP?

Those who read the first five chapters know us well enough not to expect a definitive answer to the above question. Our job, as we see it, is to explain the rules of the game (i.e., Georgia law) to the reader. Once you know how things work in Georgia, you can make an informed decision as to the type of business ownership that best accomplishes your goal.

> ## SOLE PROPRIETORSHIP
> ### Maximum control — Maximum liability

You are the boss if you do business in your name only, but you take full personal responsibility for any loss suffered by the company; and as explained, you may need to consult with an attorney if you want to make arrangements for someone to take over your business should you become incapacitated or die.

Because of this personal liability issue, many people think it best to form a corporation as soon as they start up the business. That may not be the best strategy. It takes money to form a corporation. You may need to pay an attorney to set up the corporation. You will need to pay a filing fee when you send your Articles of Incorporation to the Georgia Secretary of State. The next business day you must deliver a Notice of Incorporation along with a publication fee to the publisher of a newspaper of general circulation in the county where the company's registered office is located. Each year you need to file an annual report and pay an annual filing fee (OCG 14-2-201.1, 14-2-122). And there may be additional accounting fees. Each year you will need to file separate corporate income tax returns; one for the state and one for the IRS.

You do not need to pay filing fees to the Secretary of State to form a sole proprietorship, and you do not need to file separate income tax returns. You can include your business income as part of your personal income tax return and not go through the cost and hassle of filing a separate corporate return.

Another reason to start business as a sole proprietorship is the risk of failure. Although every new business owner thinks his venture must surely culminate in riches, research conducted by the Brandow Company shows that only 55% of new businesses get to celebrate their third birthday (see their data at www.brandow.com). You can always form a corporation should your business succeed. If the business does not succeed, then at least you didn't waste time, effort and money to form a corporation.

But What About My Personal Liability?

Many people seek to limit their personal liability by forming a corporation, however, that doesn't always work in the real world. For example, if you wish to rent a store front or office space, an experienced landlord will allow you to lease the space in the corporate name, but he will require you to sign as a guarantor. Should the business fail, he will have the right to sue you, personally, for the full value of the lease. Once you have established a successful business, the landlord may agree to just hold the business liable; and in that case having a corporation instead of a sole proprietorship will limit your personal liability.

Regardless of what form of business ownership you choose, you can be held personally liable for any fraudulent or negligent act that you commit. The way to avoid personal liability for fraudulent acts is not to willfully (deliberately) deceive or cheat anyone.

Most of us are honest folk, but negligence is another matter. We all make mistakes. The way to limit your liability for negligence is to purchase insurance that provides protection for mistakes and accidents. For example, if you open a title insurance business, you can purchase an Errors and Omissions insurance policy to cover a loss caused by a mistake you might make in a title search. If you have any business involving the care of a person (adult or child day care center, nurse practitioner, etc.), it is important to have coverage for an injury to a client due to accident or malpractice.

If you have a business location (a storefront or office) consider purchasing a comprehensive business insurance policy to cover injury to anyone who visits your business, as well as damages to the premises. For example, if you open a flower shop you can get insurance to cover an injury to a customer who slips and falls. The same policy can cover vandalism to your shop, such as a broken plate glass window. You can be compensated for loss should a storm cause the electricity to go out and your shipment of fresh cut flowers wilt for lack of refrigeration.

The purpose of any business insurance policy is to shift the risk of a business loss from your pocket to that of the insurance company.

And the downside is . . .
The problem with insurance is the greater the risk, the greater the cost. We all would like 100% insurance coverage, but few of us can afford the premium. What holds true for life insurance holds true for business insurance. The right amount of insurance coverage for you is the amount that allows you to sleep at night.

A business partnership is much like a marriage. You can both start out with the best of intentions, only to find that you are hopelessly incompatible. The break-up of a business partnership can be just as bitter and hotly contested as the breakup of a marriage. A properly drafted partnership agreement is a must — not only to set the terms of a dissolution, but to clearly state what is expected of each partner; i.e., how much each will contribute to the business venture in terms of effort or financing.

The partnership agreement should cover what will happen to the partner's share in the event of his incapacity or death. Most partnership agreements provide for an appraisal of the business and the buy out of the deceased (or disabled) partner's share. The partnership agreement may need to be backed up with financing. For example, you could sign a partnership agreement that requires the company to buy out your partnership interest should you become disabled or die. But what good is the Agreement if there is not enough cash in the company to pay for the buy out?

You will have better protection if the partnership agreement requires the company to maintain disability and life insurance to pay for the buy out. Many insurance companies offer Key man insurance. The policy is designed to compensate the company for the loss of someone who is essential to the continuation of the business. If sufficient insurance is purchased, the proceeds of the policy can be used to cover any loss suffered by the company and to buy out the share of the company that was owned by the deceased or disabled partner.

COMPANIES THAT LIMIT LIABILITY

The sole proprietorship and the partnership are the earliest type of business organization. Georgia laws governing these types of business organizations have their roots in English Common Law. Common law requires the sole proprietor and each business partner to take full personal responsibility for the debts of the company. As people became ever more litigious (lawyer talk for "sue happy") businessmen sought to limit their liability and prevailed on the legislature to create a form of business ownership to limit that liability. Legislatures in each state responded to that need by giving businessmen the right to create a company (the corporation) with an identity separate from the owners of the business. By doing business as a corporation, the businessman's liability is limited to the money he invests in the company. A person can sue the corporation for business debts, but not the owners of the corporation.

This does not mean that a corporate owner can use the corporation to do things that are fraudulent. If he does, he can be held personally liable. The owner of the corporation cannot use the corporation as a "veil" to cover his wrongdoing. Courts in Georgia have authority to disregard the corporate form and "pierce the corporate veil" in the interests of justice. But this is not easily done. The Georgia Court of Appeals ruled that in order to pierce the corporate veil it must be shown that "... the stockholders' disregard of the corporate entity made it a mere instrumentality for the transaction of their own affairs; that there is such a unity of interest and ownership that the separate personalities of the corporation and the owners no longer exist; and to adhere to the doctrine of corporate entity would promote injustice or protect fraud." (*Trans-American Communications v. Nolle*, 214 S.E.2d 717 (1975)).

THE CORPORATION
flexible control — limited liability

Whoever forms a corporation (the *incorporator*) has maximum control over the corporation. He decides how the company will operate by having the Articles of Incorporation and the company By-laws prepared according to his specifications. He can keep full control of the company as the only shareholder, or he can distribute shares and give up as much control as he wishes. Transferring corporate ownership is simple. It is a matter of signing a stock certificate transferring the shares of stock in the company. You can have a Transfer On Death designation to a named beneficiary.

If you own shares of stock in your name only, without a TOD designation, your Personal Representative will transfer the shares to the proper beneficiary. But keeping shares in your name only may not be the best way to go if you own a majority of shares and operate the business yourself. If Probate is necessary, it may take several months before the shares are transferred to the proper beneficiary, meanwhile, someone needs to continue to operate the business. If you do not leave directions for the continuation of the business, the Personal Representative (or the Probate Court) may decide it is best to just sell the company and give the proceeds of the sale to your beneficiaries.

The better route is to have your attorney prepare a Revocable Living Trust and transfer the shares into the Trust. The Trust document can give your Successor Trustee specific instructions about how the business is to be managed or transferred should you become incapacitated or die. Still another important benefit is to avoid the need to Probate what may be your only valuable asset.

THE LIMITED PARTNERSHIP

Just as a sole proprietor can limit his liability by forming a corporation, the partners of a general partnership can limit their liability by converting the partnership to a *Limited Partnership*. As with the corporation, the Limited Partnership is a creation of the legislature and is regulated by Georgia law. The name of the Limited Partnership must identify it as a limited partnership or contain the initials "L.P." A Certificate of Limited Partnership must be filed in the office of the Georgia Secretary of State (OCG 14-9-201).

The structure of a Limited Partnership differs from a general partnership. In a general partnership, each partner has full authority to conduct business on behalf of the partnership. Each partner is personally liable for monies owed by the partnership, regardless of whether that partner actually incurred the debt. The Limited Partnership has *General Partners* and *Limited Partners*. Although a Limited Partner can participate in the management and control of the company, only a General Partner is liable for company debts (OCG 14-9-303, 14-9-404).

But even a General Partner can avoid personal liability by forming a corporation, and then letting the corporation serve as the sole General Partner. An unpaid creditor of the Limited Partnership can sue the corporate General Partner, but not the shareholders of the corporation. Liability can be limited to the amount of money invested in the business venture. None of the owners will have personal liability. Of course, as with the corporation, all parties can be held personally liable for fraudulent or criminal acts performed in their partnership capacity.

The astute reader might be wondering "Why would anyone form a corporation (and pay all of the costs to set up the corporation) and then make the corporation the General Partner of a Limited Partnership (after paying all that money to set up the Partnership)? If limited business liability is the goal, why not just form a corporation?"

Answers to those questions are many and in fact, far removed from the original goal of limiting the business risk of the partners to just the money they invested in the business. The Limited Partnership can be used as a means of transferring a family business to the children with some significant tax benefits. For example, suppose Mom & Pop run a small, highly profitable, rapidly expanding, gourmet chocolate shop. They have two children, both in college. Right now, the business is worth about $500,000, but they figure that by the time they retire, the business could be worth millions. If their children inherit the business at that time, there could be significant Estate Taxes due. Also, because they are making lots of money right now, they are paying very high income taxes.

Both problems can be solved with a Family Limited Partnership. Mom and Pop can be the General Partners of the company and retain total control. They could make each child a Limited Partner by transferring shares of the business worth less than the current annual Gift Tax Exclusion. That exclusion is currently $11,000, so together Mom and Pop can gift shares of the partnership up to $22,000 per child, per year. By gifting a percentage of the business each year, the parents can eventually transfer all of the business to the children. When the parents die, there will be no Gift or Estate Tax because the children already own the business. Of course there is still the problem of the Capital Gains Tax should the children decide to sell the business.

Regardless of how much of the company they give away, Mom and Pop can keep total control of the company because they are the General Partners. When the parents are ready to retire, one or both of the children can take over as General Partner — but if making chocolate is not their thing, the parents can arrange to have a corporation manage the Limited Partnership and the children continue to receive income as limited partners. As for the current income tax problem, the children, as Limited Partners, are entitled to receive income from the business. Income paid to the children and their parents is generally taxed at a lower rate than the taxes to just Mom and Pop. For example, suppose the company earns $100,000. Mom and Pop will pay a high rate of income tax if they are the only two partners in the company.
If the children become partners, then each partner can earn $25,000 and the overall bill for income taxes will be smaller.

Still another important advantage of the Family Limited Partnership over the corporation is creditor protection for the child's partnership interest. For example, suppose one of the children becomes a dentist, gets sued for malpractice, and loses the case. Had Mom and Pop incorporated the business and given the children most of the shares of stock in the company, the creditor could take the shares to satisfy the judgment. The creditor could wind up owning the company! Not so, with a Limited Partnership interest. A judge could order that the income from the Limited Partnership be used to pay the judgment, but he could not order the Partnership share itself to be given to the creditor unless the Limited Partnership Agreement allows for such transfer or all of the partners agree (OCG 14-9-702, 14-9-703, 14-9-704). Not likely with Mom and Pop as General Partners. They might even decide to use company income to pay themselves salary and not distribute anything to the hapless creditor!

We used an actual business as an example to explain how the Limited Partnership worked. It didn't take Estate Planning attorneys long to figure out that the "family business" could be just income producing items (such as stocks and bonds) that Mom and Pop placed into the Limited Partnership. The family "business" could be just the business of earning income. In other words, the Family Limited Partnership (or even a Family Partnership) could just be a type of an Estate Plan created solely for the purpose of transferring assets to the children to avoid paying Estate Taxes, and to pay less in income taxes.

It didn't take the IRS long to challenge this method of Estate Planning. A series of IRS rulings and court cases followed, with the main issue being whether a bona fide business partnership existed.

There is a common sense rule of evidence that says "If it looks like a duck and walks like a duck, and quacks like a duck, it must be a duck." In 1946 the Supreme Court decided that whether a family partnership is really a business partnership for tax purposes, should be determined on a case by case basis; and that the IRS should use the "walk and quack" test. Only the justices said this in proper legal terms. They said to determine whether a partnership exists depends on ". . .whether the partners really and truly intended to join together for the purpose of carrying on a business and sharing in the profits or losses or both. And their intention in this respect is a question of fact, to be determined from testimony disclosed by their agreement, considered as a whole, and by their conduct in execution of its provisions" (*Commissioner v. Tower*, 327 U.S. 280 (1946)).

THE LIMITED LIABILITY COMPANY

The IRS continues to take a close look at family partnerships, and will challenge any tax break if the family partnership (limited or not) does not meet the basic requirement of being a bona fide business partnership. Perhaps in response to IRS challenges, in the 1990s each of the 50 states, and even the District of Columbia, passed laws enabling residents of their state to form a new business entity called a *Limited Liability Company* ("LLC").

This new entity is not required to be a profit making venture. In Georgia, it can be formed to carry on any lawful activity. A Limited Liability Company is formed by filing Articles of Organization with the Georgia Secretary of State (OCG 14-11-201, 14-11-203, 14-11-207).

The LLC combines the better features of the Limited Partnership and the corporation. Like the corporation, it can be formed by a single person who sets the rules of the company when he forms the corporation. The set of rules is called an *Operating Agreement*. The LLC can be run by a manager (who is not a member of the company) or it can be run by a member or members of the company. As with a corporation, all members have limited liability, regardless of whether that member happens to be managing the company; however all of the members are personally liable for taxes owed by the company.

As with a Limited Partnership, a creditor cannot take possession or control of a share of the company owned by a member as repayment of the debt. The most the creditor can do is get a court to assign income generated by that share to the creditor (OCG 14-11-303, 14-11-304, 14-11-504).

Now Mom and Pop can form a LLC, give away some or all of the shares of the company during their lifetime, and still keep control of the company, and with no more personal liability than a non-managing member of the Limited Liability Company.

Transfers into the Limited Liability Company can be made so that there are no Estate or Gift Tax consequences. Income can be distributed to the children, or not, as Mom and Pop see fit.

The skeptic is probably thinking "Maximum control, limited liability, easily transferred to my beneficiaries, no Estate Tax. This is too good to be true. There must be a catch somewhere."

And so there is. It's called the Capital Gains Tax. If you transfer property during your lifetime, that property is valued by the IRS as of the date of transfer. If you gift a share of the Limited Liability Company during your lifetime, your beneficiary will take your basis in the property (i.e., the value that you paid for your interest in the Company). If you sell the share to your beneficiary, his basis is the fair market value of the share as of the date of purchase. Either way, once the beneficiary decides to sell the property, there may be a significant Capital Gains Tax due.

An experienced Estate Planning attorney should be able to suggest any number of ways to solve the problem, including purchasing life insurance to pay the tax.

INSURANCE TO PAY DEBTS AND TAXES

Regardless of what form of business ownership you have, you need to think about what will happen to your business in the event of your incapacity or death. And in particular, how company debts will be paid. If your business is highly leveraged (business talk for "owes lots of money"), you also need to consider how those loans will be paid should you become disabled or die. One solution is to purchase Key man insurance. As explained earlier, Key man insurance is protection for the company against the loss of a valuable employee. The company purchases the policy and the proceeds are paid to the company to compensate it for the loss; but ultimately the policy benefits those who inherit the business.

Taxes are still another concern. Your business may be worth millions on paper, and your Estate Taxes will be based on that value. Your heirs might be forced to sell the company just to pay the taxes, but without your leadership they may get only a fraction of the value of the company.

Even if the federal government decides to eliminate federal Estate Taxes, the state of Georgia, or any other state where you have a business location, may decide to levy an Estate or Inheritance Tax.

And there is still the problem of the Capital Gains Tax. No one in Congress is talking about doing away with the Capital Gains Tax — and that tax could be sizeable. One solution to the problem of an unknown Estate Tax and/or Capital Gains Tax is to purchase life insurance that can be used to pay for any Estate Tax that may be due upon your death and any Capital Gains Tax that may be due when your beneficiary sells the property he inherits.

That may sound like a good, simple, solution, but you need to think things through before calling your insurance agent. The first question being:

How much insurance should I purchase?
That is a tough question. If you are in good health, who knows what will happen before you die. Will your business increase in value or go bust? Will the federal government really do away with Estate Taxes or will they do nothing and allow the tax to be reinstated in 2011?

The last question is particularly troublesome. Under today's tax law, if you purchase a life insurance policy, or even control the benefits of the policy, all of the proceeds of the policy will be counted as part of your taxable Estate. You may be buying insurance just to pay more in taxes to Uncle Sam.

You don't need a soothsayer or psychic to solve the problem. A financial planner with access to computer generated models can predict your life expectancy, how much your business will be worth when you retire and even the probability that the economy will require Estate taxes to be reinstated!

Suppose your financial planner predicts that between federal and Georgia Estate Taxes your heirs will probably need to pay one million dollars in taxes. If you purchase a million dollar insurance policy, the value of the policy will be included in your Estate. If Estates are taxed at 40% your heirs will net only $600,000 of your million dollar policy, the rest going for Estate Taxes on the proceeds of the policy itself. Your heirs will need to come up with an additional $400,000 to make up for the original million dollars predicted as being necessary to pay your Estate Taxes. The solution to this dilemma is the IRREVOCABLE LIFE INSURANCE TRUST.

THE IRREVOCABLE LIFE INSURANCE TRUST

An *Irrevocable Life Insurance Trust* can be designed to provide money to pay any tax that may be due after your death. To be sure that the IRS does not count the proceeds of the Trust as part of your taxable Estate the Trust must meet the following requirements:

⇨ The Trust must be irrevocable.

⇨ You cannot be Trustee.

The Trust can be set up for the benefit of your child. In such case, the child can be Trustee of the Trust. The child, as Trustee, will purchase an insurance policy on your life. You may need to file a Gift Tax return if you give your child a large sum of money to purchase the policy. It is better to have the child purchase a policy that is paid in quarterly or annual premiums instead of a single lump sum payment. You can give the child an amount each year up to the Annual Gift Tax Exclusion (currently $11,000) to pay for the premium. If you are married, you and your spouse can gift up to $22,000 per year without the need to file a Gift Tax return.

As tax laws change, the child/Trustee can use as much of the gift as is needed to purchase sufficient insurance to cover the taxes. The Trust can be set up to cover Estate Taxes or Capital Gains Taxes, or both. For example, the Trustee can purchase an insurance policy that pays a million dollars upon your death. Those insurance funds can be used to pay your Estate Taxes. Should it happen that no Estate Taxes is due, the Trustee can keep the monies invested until the business is sold. The Trust funds can be used to pay any Capital Gains Tax that may be due at that time. If monies are left over once all taxes are paid, they can be distributed to the named beneficiaries of the Trust.

Your attorney can design an Irrevocable Insurance Trust in any number of ways to meet the special needs of you and your family. For example, an Irrevocable Insurance Trust can be set up to solve problems described in the last Chapter. Alan wanted to leave insurance proceeds for his child but was concerned that the cash value of the policy could be taken by his creditors. A properly drafted Irrevocable Insurance Trust can solve such problem, because the Trust, and not Alan, is the owner of the policy.

Of course, it costs significant money to set up and maintain an Irrevocable Insurance Trust. Those who do not have concerns about creditors may wonder whether it's necessary to go through all that cost and bother if there will be no more Estate Taxes in the future. After all a simple life insurance policy can cover any Capital Gains Tax that may be due. But, as explained, the tax law as passed in 2001 reinstates the Estate Tax in 2011. If lawmakers take no further action, the Estate of anyone who dies on January 1, 2011, and thereafter is subject to an Estate Tax for an Estate over one million dollars.

Someone with an active imagination could envision the following scenario:

It is New Year's eve, 2010. A 97 year old lies sleeping, at his home, surrounded by his four grandchildren who are his sole heirs.

"He looks so peaceful."

"Yes. Surprising, considering that he has terminal cancer, failing kidneys and heart. His doctor says he can't last more than a few days. The doctor left a supply of morphine so that we can keep Gramps comfortable over the New Year's holiday. The doctor gave him a shot just before he left."

"The doctor said not to give Gramps another shot unless he was in pain. His heart is in such a weakened condition, he could easily overdose on morphine."

"Yes, of course."

"Too bad he didn't get a chance to do some Estate Planning before he had that stroke last year. "

"I thought his attorney took care of all that."

"His attorney suggested he set up an Irrevocable Insurance Trust to pay for any Estate Tax, but Gramps felt sure that Congress would pass a law that would permanently repeal the Estate Tax."

"I can't imagine Gramps coming to that conclusion. The economy is down and the government needs to raise taxes. It is easier for legislators to leave the law as written back in 2001, than take some affirmative action."

"Gramps was always a sharp business man, but in his later years his mind wasn't as clear as when he earned his five million dollars."

"Is that what we are going to inherit?"

"Not unless he dies before midnight. After midnight the Estate Tax is reinstated, and at a rate of 45%. Between state and federal taxes, we'll be lucky to come away with half a mill each."

"Gramps moved. I think he may be in pain."

"Yes, he does look uncomfortable."

"It isn't right to let him suffer like this."

"Yes, of course."

Continuing To Care 7

There are any number of reasons that people give for wanting to continue on with their lives. For the lucky ones, their main reason for living is that they are having a great time and don't want it to end. For many, it is more a sense of responsibility. During child rearing years the concern of the parent is what will happen to the child should the parent suddenly die. Once a child is grown, the roles often reverse, and it is the child worrying about what will happen to his parent if the child were not present to see to the care of the aging parent. Even pet lovers worry about what will happen to their pet should the owner no longer be around.

There is little that can be done to prepare those who depend on you for the loss of your companionship and emotional support; but there are many things you can do to provide financial support for those who rely on you. Even people of modest means can make financial provision so their loved ones will have an easy transition from being dependent to becoming self sufficient.

This chapter explains the many simple, and relatively inexpensive, things you can do to provide care for your loved ones should you not be present to do so yourself.

CARING FOR THE MINOR CHILD

It doesn't happen very often, but both parents could die or become incapacitated before their child reaches adulthood. Most parents don't want to think about, much less prepare for such a happening. But in this age of postponing parenthood, many parents are in their fifties and sixties and still raising children. The probability of a life threatening illness increases with age, so parents need to understand the importance of planning ahead.

Parents with dangerous occupations also need to provide for the care of their minor child in the event of the disability or death of both parents. It is surprising to think of how many of us are employed in dangerous occupations. Construction workers, military personnel, firemen, state and federal law enforcement agents, and in this day and age, even postal workers face hazards on a daily basis.

Regardless of the parent's age or occupation, planning for the care of a minor child should be part of every parent's Estate Plan, not only because it is the responsible thing to do, but also because it is relatively simple and inexpensive to do.

A child must be cared for in two ways, the *person* of the child and the *Estate* (i.e., property) of the child. To care for the person of the child, someone must be in charge of the child's everyday living, not only food and shelter but also to provide social, ethical and religious training. Someone must have legal authority to make medical decisions and see to the child's education. To care for the child's Estate, someone must be responsible to see that monies left to the child are used for the care of the child and that anything left over is preserved until the child becomes an adult.

A Guardian will need to be appointed to care for the person of the child in the event that both parents become incapacitated or die before the child is grown.

USING A WILL TO APPOINT A GUARDIAN

As explained in Chapter 4, each parent can use his/her Will to appoint someone to serve as Guardian of their minor child in the event that both parents die before the child is grown.

It is a good idea for both parents to name the same person to serve as Guardian. If the child's parents appoint different people for the job and then die simultaneously, it will be up to the judge to decide who is best suited to be Guardian. If they do not die simultaneously, the Court will give top priority to the person named in the Will of the last parent to die (OCG 29-4-3).

One problem with using a Will to appoint someone to be your child's Guardian, is that for the appointment to be effective, the Will must be admitted to Probate; i.e., the Court must determine that the Will is valid; and the person you chose as Guardian needs to file a petition to be appointed as the child's Guardian. It might take several weeks before that person has the legal authority to care for the child. A better solution is to appoint someone as a **STANDBY GUARDIAN** who can immediately assume responsibility for the care of the minor child, should the need arise.

APPOINTING A STANDBY GUARDIAN

Appointing a Standby Guardian is easily done by signing the statutory form of the *Designation of Standby Guardian* (OCG 29-2-11). The form can be copied at any law library or downloaded from the Georgia Statute Web site.
http://www.legis.state.ga.us

Both parents need to sign the Designation of Standby Guardian in the presence of two witnesses. Only one signature is required if the other parent is deceased, or has had his parental rights terminated, or is missing and cannot be found. The Standby Guardian will need to sign the document as well. Appointing a Standby Guardian does not change the right of the parent to care for the child while the parent is able to do so. The appointment of a Standby Guardian becomes effective only when both parents are unable to care for their child or are deceased. The parent is free to revoke the Designation at any time during his lifetime (OCG 29-2-10, 29-2-12).

The Standby Guardian can immediately take over the care of the child in the event both parents are incapacitated or deceased, but within four months the Standby Guardian must petition to be appointed as the legal Guardian of the minor. If the Standby Guardian does not apply to be Guardian within that time, the Court may appoint someone else for the job (OCG 29-2-13).

Even healthy parents should consider signing a Designation of Standby Guardian for their minor child. It is surprising to think how many of us are employed in hazardous occupations such as policeman, fireman, construction worker, member of the armed forces — and even postal employees.

Many parents never get around to appointing a Guardian for their minor child because they cannot come to an agreement as to the best choice of Guardian. "I think my mother should be Guardian. After all she raised me, and I turned out fine" can signal the opening salvo of a lengthy, and often unresolved battle. Not being able to agree on a choice of Guardian should not discourage you from appointing the person of your choice either as part of your Will or in a separate writing.

The thing to keep in mind is that the Guardian of your choice will take over only if the other parent is deceased or incapacitated. Even if you both die simultaneously, and you each name someone different to serve as Guardian, your choice of Guardian will at least be brought to the attention of the Court.

It is important that the person you choose to serve as Guardian be compatible with the child. If your choice of Guardian is not that of the child's, and the child is at least 14, he can ask the Court to appoint the Guardian of his choice. If the Court finds that person to be qualified, the Court will appoint the person chosen by the child to serve as his Guardian (OCG 29-2-20).

If neither parent has expressed his choice of Guardian, and the child is under 14, the choice of Guardian will be that of the Court. He will base his choice on the interest of the child.

As any parent is well aware, it is expensive to raise a child. The person you consider to be the best choice to serve as Guardian might not be able to do so unless you leave sufficient monies to pay for the care of the child. If you have limited finances, consider purchasing a term life insurance policy on your life and/or on the life of the other parent of the child. If you can only afford one policy, insure the life of the parent who contributes most to the support of the child.

Term insurance policies are relatively inexpensive if you limit the term to just that period of time until your child becomes an adult. Some companies offer a combination of term life and disability insurance, in the event that the bread-winner becomes disabled and unable to work. As with any other purchase, it is important to comparison shop to obtain the best price for the coverage.

If you are married, you may want to name your spouse as the beneficiary of the term insurance policy with your child as an alternate beneficiary. Married or single, you can name your child as the primary beneficiary of the policy. The insurance company can transfer up to $15,000 to the parent of the child, provided the parent signs an *Affidavit* (a written statement sworn to before a Notary Public) saying that all of the personal property of the minor does not exceed $15,000 and no Conservator has been appointed for the minor (OCG 29-3-1).

But the insurance company is not required to make the transfer even for amounts under $15,000. They may require a Court order before transferring any sum to the parent.

We discussed the ways parents can control who is appointed to serve as the Guardian of their minor child should both parents be incapacitated or deceased. Guardianship is a necessity in such cases. But if at least one of the parents is able to care for the person of the child, it may be wise to avoid the need for the Court to appoint a Conservator for the child's property. If you leave the child a significant amount of money that's what the Court will do. Even if the surviving parent is appointed to serve as Conservator, the amount you leave to the child will be reduced by the cost of establishing and maintaining the conservatorship.

An attorney must be employed to establish the conservatorship. Once appointed, the Conservator must prepare an inventory and file an annual accounting with the Court. The Conservator may need to employ an accountant to assist with the preparation of the inventory and the annual accounting. Depending on the size of the Estate, the Guardian of the property may need to employ a financial advisor to manage the property. All these people are entitled to be paid. Their fees are proper charges to the child's Estate (OCG 29-3-50, 29-3-51, 29-3-60).

Monies left for the care of the child may be significantly reduced by the cost of caring for the property. This can be avoided by leaving property to the child in such a manner that will make it unnecessary for the Court to appoint a Conservator. One way to do so is to include a Trust for the child as part of your Will. Another is to set up a Revocable Living Trust that includes provisions for the care of the child. If you have limited finances, a good alternative is to appoint someone to serve as Custodian of the gift under the GEORGIA TRANSFERS TO MINORS ACT.

THE TRANSFERS TO MINORS ACT

The *Georgia Transfers to Minors Act* is designed to protect gifts made to a minor by appointing someone to be the *Custodian* of a gift until the child is an adult. For example, you can make a minor child the beneficiary of your life insurance policy, and name a trusted relative or friend or even a financial institution to be the Custodian of the gift. Should you die while the child is a minor, the insurance company will give the proceeds of the policy to the person you named as Custodian to hold until the child is an adult.

You can make a gift to a minor in your Will. You can appoint your Personal Representative (or anyone else) as Custodian of the gift. For example:

I give the sum of $20,000 to _____(name) as custodian for _____ (name of minor) under the Georgia Transfers to Minors Act.

THE LIFETIME GIFT

You can even use the Georgia Transfers to Minors Act to make a gift during your lifetime of some item such as shares in a corporation or a limited partnership interest. You can nominate yourself as Custodian of the gift, or you can name another person to serve as Custodian. Once the lifetime gift is made it becomes irrevocable, so this method is not appropriate unless you are sure that you want the child to have the gift once he/she is an adult.

In general, the Custodian must distribute the gift when the child reaches 18; however, if you make a lifetime gift, or a gift as part of your Will, you can direct the Custodian to distribute the gift when the child reaches 21 (OCG 44-5-114, 44-5-119, 44-5-130).

THE CUSTODIAN'S DUTIES

Under Georgia law, while the Custodian is in possession of the gift, he can use as much of the gift as he thinks advisable for the benefit of the child. He can pay monies directly to the child, or use the funds for the child's benefit. In making the distribution he is not obliged to take into account that someone else has a duty to support the child — even if the Custodian is the child's parent and it is his own responsibility to support the child (OCG 44-5-124).

The Custodian can do the opposite and distribute nothing. He can refuse to use any of the monies for the child and just keep the funds invested until the child is 21. In such case, the child's parent or guardian (or even the child once he is 14) can ask a Court to order that the monies be used for the care of the child. The judge will determine what is in the child's best interest and then rule on the matter.

The Custodian is required to keep records of all custodial transactions. Hopefully, the Custodian will give a regular accounting to the child's parent or Guardian. If not, any member of the child's family, or the child once he/she reaches 14, can ask the Court to order a full accounting of the custodial property (OCG 44-5-122, 45-5-129).

As with any type of Estate Plan, you need to examine all aspects of the transfer to see if there is anything that may be objectionable to you.

THE CUSTODIAN'S FEE

The law requires the Custodian to invest and manage the property in a responsible, prudent manner. The Custodian is entitled to be paid for his effort. If the gift is sizeable, his fee can be sizeable. Before appointing a person or a financial institution as Custodian, it is best to come to a written agreement about how the property will be managed and the charge for doing so (OCG 44-5-125).

NO GROUP GIFT

You cannot make a gift to more than one child under the Georgia Transfers To Minors Act. For example, you cannot make a single gift of real property to two or more minor children under the Transfers To Minors Act. If you wanted to make such a gift, you would need to do so by another method, such as creating a Trust for the children (OCG 44-5-120).

THE COST OF PROBATE

As discussed, you can include a gift to a minor in your Will by naming a Custodian for the gift. As with any gift made under a Will, a Probate procedure will be necessary to distribute the gift to the Custodian. If you are trying to avoid Probate, then this may not be the best way to go. If your gift is significant, the better route is to set up a Revocable Living Trust. You can manage the Trust while you are able. Should you become incapacitated or die before the child is grown your Successor Trustee will take over. Unlike the Georgia Transfers To Minors Act, you can direct the Trustee to give the gift to the child at any age you think proper.

Which brings us to another problem, namely, that there is no flexibility as to the final distribution of a gift made under the Georgia Transfers To Minors Act.

MANDATORY DISTRIBUTION

A Custodian appointed under the Georgia Transfers To Minors Act must distribute the gift by the child's 18th birthday (21st if your Will or lifetime gift so directs) (OCG 44-5-130). The gift must be made regardless of whether the child has sufficient maturity to handle the money in a responsible manner. A sizeable gift to an immature beneficiary is not the best Estate Plan.

PROVIDING FOR THE STEPCHILD

Perhaps the reason that the story of Cinderella has such universal appeal is that many stepchildren, at one point or another, feel left out. The law seems to reinforce that perception. Unless a married person makes provision otherwise, a spouse has priority over the child in health matters both before and after death. If a married person is too ill to make medical decisions, the doctors will turn to the spouse for directions. Should a married person die, the decedent's spouse and not the child, has the authority to agree to an autopsy or anatomical gift (OCG 21-9-2, 44-5-143).

If a married couple hold all of their property jointly, that property will go to the surviving spouse and not to the child of the deceased parent. This might not be a problem if the surviving spouse is the natural parent of the child. It could be a major problem if the natural parent dies first. The stepchild of the surviving parent may be left with nothing.

In such situations, the stepparent comes across as villain, but it is the parent, and not the stepparent, who decides whether the child will inherit property belonging to the natural parent. Too often the stepchild is left out by default, i.e., the natural parent doesn't give the matter any thought, or perhaps the natural parent is confident that the stepparent will do "what's right."

That was the case with Walter. He always wanted to be a father, so he was pleased when Todd was born just before the first anniversary of Walter's marriage to Nancy. Twin girls were born just 15 months later. Unfortunately the twins' birth was premature, causing them to have medical and developmental problems. Nancy had her hands full just caring for the three children, so it was up to Walter to support the family.

Walter was up to the job. He was both conscientious and ambitious. He started his own interior decorating business, complete with a retail sales storefront to sell fabrics, and an upholstery shop in the rear of the store. With hard work and long hours, he was able to make a comfortable living. But the strain of raising a family and running a business took its toll, both on him and the marriage. At 40, he felt like an old man.

All that changed when he hired Annie to manage the retail part of his business. Her energy and sunny disposition were just what the business (and Walter) needed.

Walter's divorce from Nancy was amicable. Walter was a loving father who took his responsibilities seriously. He was generous when it came to supporting the children. Walter had only finished high school, and he wanted more for his son. He encouraged Todd to do well in school so that he could go on to college, and maybe become a doctor or lawyer. The twins had developmental problems; but Walter encouraged them to reach their maximum potential. It was his goal to help them become self sufficient.

Annie got along very well with her stepchildren. She had no trouble with Walter's desire to support the children and give them a good start in life. Even though they held all of their money in a joint account, she never questioned any expense made on behalf of the children.

Walter never gave much thought to an Estate Plan. After all, he was healthy, and in the prime of his earning capacity. He often said that he was fortunate to have married two wonderful women. If he had a dark thought, it soon passed, rationalizing that if something happened to him, Annie would take care of the children.

But she didn't.

Walter died in one of those freak accidents. He was trimming the branches from his tree with an electric saw and accidentally touched an overhead wire. All he owned was tied up in the business that he held jointly with Annie. Annie felt that she was a major factor in the success of that business. Why should she share any of her hard earned money with Nancy? As for the children, it was Nancy's job to raise them. After all they were Nancy's children, and not Annie's. If it was a struggle to support the children, then that was Nancy's problem!

A better argument (but one she didn't raise) was that Walter really wanted Annie to inherit everything. If he wanted to provide for his children, he could have done so in any number of different ways, beginning with his marriage to Annie:

✍   He could have insisted on a prenuptial agreement that would have provided for certain funds to be kept separate for the benefit of his children.

✍   He could have signed a partnership agreement with Annie that would have given his share of the business to his children, in the event of his death.

✍   If he didn't want to negotiate with Annie about a prenuptial agreement or a partnership agreement, he could have had his attorney prepare a Trust that would have cared for the children until they were old enough to be on their own.

✍   If nothing else, he could have purchased a life insurance policy with the children as beneficiaries of the policy.

THE SECOND MARRIAGE TRUST

Walter's situation is not unique. Second marriages are commonplace in America. Many who are widowed or divorced, remarry. If children are involved, the parent may have divided loyalties. The parent may want to provide income to the child until the child completes his education, and then leave whatever is left of his Estate to his surviving spouse. More often it is the other way around. The parent wants to be sure that the surviving spouse has sufficient income to support his/her current life-style, but once the surviving spouse dies, the parent wants all that remains to go to his children. A properly drafted Trust can provide for the care of a spouse and child in whatever way the Grantor of the Trust thinks best.

That was the case with an elderly widower who married a pretty girl less than half his age. Their prenuptial agreement made it clear that all his property would go to his son from his first marriage. Surprisingly, the marriage turned out well. So well that the couple had two daughters. The husband decided to divide his Estate equally between his three children and to provide for the care of his wife until the youngest child was grown.

His attorney suggested a Trust. "You can be Trustee during your lifetime. Once you die, your Successor Trustee can immediately distribute one-third of the Trust to your son who is now 55. No sense to keep him waiting. The rest of your money can remain in your Trust. Income from the Trust can be used to support your wife and children until the youngest is 25. Then, whatever remains in the Trust can be distributed equally to your daughters."

"Good idea" said the elderly gentlemen, with a smile "Just make sure it is revocable during my lifetime. Who knows what adventures I might be up to in the future?"

It isn't just stepchildren who can be left out if no provision is made. Even children from a long-standing marriage can be cut off against the wishes of a parent. A parent may assume that all of their children will be treated equally when both parents are gone, but if all their property is held jointly, the last parent to die is the one who gets to decide "who gets what." Too often, the wishes of the deceased parent are ignored, for example:

THE STRAINED RELATIONSHIP A child may have a close relationship with one parent, and a strained, but tolerable, relationship with the other. Peace in the family is achieved because the parent who is close to the child acts as a buffer. Should the buffer parent die first, the relationship between the surviving parent and the child may fall apart altogether and the child's inheritance be cut off.

THE PARENT WITH DIMINISHED CAPACITY The more common scenario, is that the surviving parent becomes increasingly dependent on one child — either for emotional support, or for physical assistance as the parent ages. The other children may live at a distance, or perhaps they are too involved with their own family to assist. The supporting child may end up with most, if not all, of what was intended for all of the children.

These problems can be avoided by having your attorney prepare a Family Trust. The family assets are placed in the Trust with the parents as co-Trustees. The beneficiaries of the Trust cannot be changed unless both parents agree to the change. Once one parent dies, the Trust becomes irrevocable. The Trust income goes to the surviving parent and once that parent dies, whatever remains in the Trust is distributed in the manner as was agreed by both parents.

The caregiver of someone who is incapacitated, or developmentally disabled needs to, as part of his Estate Plan, provide for the care of the incapacitated person as well as himself. Should the caregiver become disabled or die, someone will need to take over and make medical decisions for the incapacitated person and see to it that he/she is properly housed and fed.

An aging parent of a developmentally disabled child may worry about how the child will manage without the parent to oversee his care. An aged spouse caring for his incapacitated spouse, may be concerned about who will care for the ill spouse should he die first. Often a family member will agree to take responsibility for the care of an incapacitated person; but perhaps no one wants the job.

If there are large sums of money involved it may be the opposite case, too many people may want to be in control. One family member may want the incapacitated child or spouse to remain at home with the assistance of a home health care worker. Another may think the best place is an assisted living facility with 24 hour care. The caregiver may be concerned that a tug-of-war will erupt once he dies.

In such case, the caregiver should consult with an attorney to ensure future care for the incapacitated person. The attorney may suggest that a guardianship be established to care for the ill spouse with the caregiver and his choice of successor caregiver serving as Co-Guardians. The Co-Guardian can take full responsibility for the job should the caregiver become disabled or die. Once the guardianship is in place, the Court will continue to supervise the care of the incapacitated person until he/she is restored to capacity or dies.

The attorney may suggest having a Conservator appointed to care for the property of the disabled spouse or child. The only problem with setting up a guardianship and/or conservatorship while the caregiver is able to care for the disabled spouse or child is the cost of the procedure. It may cost hundreds, if not thousands, of dollars to set up and maintain the guardianship/conservatorship. If the incapacitated person is without funds, the caregiver can ask the Legal Services for assistance in having a Guardian appointed. See page xiii for information about finding the nearest Legal Services office.

Those who have adequate funds may hesitate to go through the effort and expense to set up a guardianship if it may not be needed for years to come. An alternative is for the caregiver to make provision in his Will for the appointment of a Guardian. The parent of a disabled child or the spouse of an incapacitated person may use his Will to appoint a Guardian and/or Conservator (OCG 29-4-3, 29-5-3). Once the caregiver is deceased and the Will admitted to Probate, the Guardian named in the Will can apply to be appointed as the legal Guardian of the incapacitated person.

Before making the appointment the Court will need to establish that the person is in fact incapacitated and in need of a Guardian and/or Conservator. Establishing the need for the guardianship may take several weeks. To avoid any lapse in the care of the incapacitated person, the person named in the Will can ask the Court to be appointed as the *Emergency Guardian/Conservator*. Once the need is established, the Court can confirm the appointment and name that person as the legal Guardian or Conservator of the property of the incapacitated person (OCG 29-4-12, 29-5-6).

Those who read Chapter 2 might think a Trust can eliminate the need for a Conservator; but the problem with establishing a Trust for the incapacitated person is the possible loss of government benefits. Government assistance is available to provide medical and custodial care for those who are disabled and without the means to care for themselves. Both state and federal government provide such assistance with programs such as Social Security disability benefits, Supplemental Security Income and Medicaid.

The family often supplements the government program by providing for the incapacitated person's *supplemental needs* such as hobbies, special education, outings to a movie or a sports event — things that give the incapacitated person some quality of life. This is not a problem while family members are alive and able to provide for the incapacitated person. The worry is how to continue meeting those needs should the provider die.

To be eligible for some government assistance programs the incapacitated person must essentially be without funds. Family members fear that leaving money to the incapacitated in a Will or Trust will disqualify the incapacitated person from receiving government assistance. Parents of a disabled child may decide to solve the problem by leaving the money to a sibling or other family member with verbal instructions to take care of the child once the parent is deceased.

The problem with that approach is that once the funds are left to the family member, they become the property of the family member. As the property of the family member, they are available to his creditors. The funds could be lost in a divorce, or the family member could die and the funds inherited by someone who is not willing to care for the disabled child.

Understanding the problem, the federal and state legislature passed laws allowing the establishment of a COMMUNITY TRUST (42 USC 1396p(d)(4)(C),OCG 30-10-1, 30-10-2, 30-10-3).

A COMMUNITY TRUST FOR THE DISABLED

The *Georgia Community Trust* is a non-profit organization that qualifies as tax-exempt status under section 501(c)(3) of the Internal Revenue Code. It has a Board of Trustees that administers the Trust. Parents can contribute money to the Trust to be used for the benefit of their disabled child. The parent can serve as Advisory Co-Trustee to spend the money they donate to meet the child's supplemental needs. The parent can name someone to serve as Successor Advisory Co-Trustee, in the event that the parent becomes disabled or dies.

Upon the death of the disabled child, the remaining funds contributed by the parent will be returned to the parent or distributed to a beneficiary named by the parent. If you wish to establish an account with the Georgia Community Trust, it is important that you seek the counsel of an experienced Elder Law attorney to assist you.

You can find more information about the Community Trust on the Internet.

 GEORGIA COMMUNITY TRUST
http://www.georgiacommunitytrust.com

THE COMMUNITY TRUST FOR A DISABLED SPOUSE

The caregiver spouse can contribute funds to the Community Trust to be used for the supplemental needs of his/her disabled spouse, however, rules for a disabled spouse differ significantly from the rules for a disabled child. If the disabled person is receiving Medicaid, any contribution made with his funds or that of his spouse becomes an irrevocable transfer. The spouse may not serve as Advisory Co-Trustee. The Board of Trustees can use the donated funds to provide for the special needs of the incapacitated person, provided that whatever money remains in the Trust after the incapacitated person dies, is used to reimburse the state for monies spent on his/her behalf, or the funds are donated to a Successor Trust to benefit disabled indigent residents of Georgia (42 U.S.C. 1396p(d)(4)(C), OCG 30-10-6, 30-10-7).

This presents a dilemma. If the caregiver spouse contributes too little, there may not be sufficient funds to provide for the supplemental needs of his incapacitated spouse. If he makes too large a donation, the state will use the funds as reimbursement for the care given by the state.

In Chapter 10, we will discuss how a married couple can arrange their finances to provide for the care of a disabled spouse without jeopardizing the right of the incapacitated person to qualify for medical assistance.

CARING FOR YOUR PET

A woman died at peace,
leaving her fortune
and care of her cat to her niece.
Alas, the fortune and the cat
disappeared soon after that.

You could leave money to someone with the understanding that the person will take care of your pet, but the moral of the above limerick, is that just leaving money will not guarantee care for your pet. The better route is to have your attorney prepare a Will that includes specific instructions and funds to provide for the care of your pet during its lifetime. Those with a Trust can include a similar provision as part of the Trust. The provision for your pet should include directions saying how the remaining funds are to be distributed after the death of the pet.

A TRUST TO CARE FOR YOUR PET

If you are financially able and have several pets, you may want to set up a special Trust for the care of your pets. The person you name as Trustee will be charged with the duty to use Trust funds to pay for the care of those animals who survive you.

You also need to name a residuary beneficiary (a person or perhaps a charitable organization) to receive whatever remains in the Trust once all of the animals are deceased. Animal support groups, such as the Humane Society, have people who will care for the pet of a deceased owner. You might consider appointing such group as the remainder beneficiary of the Trust in exchange for the lifetime care of your pet(s).

If you don't have the resources to set up a Trust to care for your pet, you can still ask a fellow pet lover to care for the animal. If no one among your circle of family and friends is able to do so, then ask your pet's veterinarian to consider starting an "Orphaned Pet Service" to assist in finding new homes for pets who lose their owners. It is good public relations and a potential source of income. If this is agreeable to the Veterinarian, you can make arrangements in your Will to pay the Vet to care for the pet until a suitable family can be found. This is a more humane approach than the, all too common practice, of putting a pet "to sleep" rather than have the pet suffer the loss of its master. And in at least one case, that reasoning backfired.

Eleanor always had a pet in the house. After her husband died, her two poodles were her constant companions. When Eleanor became ill with cancer, she worried about what would happen to her "buddies" without her to care for them. She finally decided it best to have her family put them to sleep when she died.

Eleanor endured surgery, chemotherapy, radiation therapy, and even some holistic remedies, but she continued to go downhill. Eleanor's family came in to visit her at the hospital to say their last good-byes. She was so ill, she didn't even recognize them. No one thought she could last the day. Because the family was from out of state, and time short, they decided to put the pets to sleep so they need only take care of the funeral arrangements when she died.

To everyone's surprise, Eleanor rallied. She lived two more long, lonely years.

She often said she wished they had put her to sleep instead of her buddies.

THE CHARITABLE TRUST

We explained how a Trust can be set up to care for a pet and whatever is left over (the remainder) given to a charitable organization. There are other kinds of charitable trusts that can be set up to benefit the giver as well as the receiver. For example, suppose you own stock which has appreciated substantially over the years, but pays few dividends. This hasn't been a problem in the past because you earned a good income. But now you wish to retire, and will need additional income. You would like to cash in the stock and invest the funds in something that can supplement your retirement income, but your accountant says that a significant portion of the value of the stock will go to Uncle Sam as payment for the Capital Gains Tax.

By now you know that a clever Estate Planning attorney will have any number of ways to solve the problem. The dialogue with your attorney might go something like this:

ATTORNEY: "Do you have a favorite charity?"

"Yes, why do you ask?"

ATTORNEY: "You can set up a Charitable Remainder Trust and donate the stock to that charity by depositing the stock in the Trust. Charities don't pay taxes, so the stock can be sold and the proceeds invested in property that produces a good income. In return for the donation, you can receive an income for the next 20 years or you can receive a monthly annuity based on your life expectancy."

"What's in it for the charity?"

ATTORNEY: "The charity gets whatever is left after paying you the annuity."

"Yes, but suppose I die next year, and my wife is left without the securities and no income."

ATTORNEY: "No problem. If you decide on a 20 year annuity, you can name your wife or any other beneficiary to receive the balance of the annuity. If you wish, you can have an annuity based on your life expectancy and that of your spouse. If you predecease your spouse, then the income continues until she dies."

"It seems to me that if the annuity is based on my life expectancy <u>AND</u> my wife's life expectancy, there won't be much left for the charity."

ATTORNEY: "How much is left for the charity depends on the value of the gift and the cost of the annuity. The cost of the annuity depends on the combined life expectancy of you and your wife. I think the best way to understand this plan is for you to look at actual numbers. There are any number of ways to set up a Charitable Remainder Trust. I can explain each option to you. For each option, I will give you the cost of setting up the program; the amount of money you will get, and how much money will actually go to your favorite ch arity. Of course it must be an IRS approved charity. Once you see the numbers you can make an informed decision as to whether you want to sell the stock and pay the Capital Gains Tax, or set up a Charitable Trust and receive an income."

"Good idea."

Up till now Estate Planning for the wealthy was all about the Estate Tax. Estate Planning attorneys would spend their time dreaming up different ways to reduce Estate Taxes for their wealthy clients. The IRS would spend their time examining and challenging any Estate plan that appeared too innovative. It seems likely that by 2010 the federal Estate Tax will be a memory. Is the game over?

Hardly. As explained in Chapter 3, instead of paying an Estate Tax, the child who inherits property that has appreciated more than 1.3 million dollars will pay a substantial Capital Gains Tax when he sells the property. In a way, that makes sense. A major criticism of the Estate Tax was that the tax had to be paid within 9 months of the date of death. That created a hardship for those inheriting a small business with a high assessed value but with no cash to pay taxes on that value.

Critics of the Estate Tax often cited the example of the cash poor farm located on valuable land. Once the owner of the farm died, the family would be forced to sell the farm just to pay Estate Taxes. By substituting the Capital Gains tax for the Estate Tax, that problem is eliminated. No Capital Gains Tax need be paid until the beneficiary decides to sell the property. Theoretically, the family farm can now be inherited generation to generation with no tax consequence.

But there are few family farms in today's economy. Future heirs are more likely to inherit highly appreciated real property or securities that they will eventually want to sell. And when they do, they may need to pay a significant Capital Gains Tax. In Georgia Capital Gains is taxed as ordinary income; so the resident of Georgia will pay taxes on the Capital Gain to the federal government and to the state of Georgia, as well (OCG 48-7-27).

The new game for Estate Planning attorneys will be to devise an Estate Plan that will reduce the Capital Gains Tax. The IRS will, no doubt, enjoy challenging those plans.

One tried (and legal) method of reducing the Capital Gains Tax is the Charitable Remainder Trust as was just discussed. It doesn't take a crystal ball to see that this could well be the basis of future Estate Plans, so we will take a few more pages to describe the pros and cons of the Trust.

THE CHARITABLE REMAINDER ANNUITY TRUST

A *Charitable Remainder Annuity Trust* is a Trust that is established according to the Internal Revenue Code (IRC 664). Charities do not pay taxes, so property donated to the Trust can be sold by the Trustee free of the Capital Gains Tax. Money from the sale is invested so that it provides an income (an *annuity*) to the beneficiary (the *annuitant*) for a fixed period of time, say 20 years, or for the annuitant's lifetime as computed by actuarial tables (i.e., life expectancy tables). The charity receives whatever is left (the *remainder*) after payment of the annuity. How much income the donor will receive and how much the charity will receive, is agreed upon at the time the Trust is set up.

The Trust can be set up in any number of ways depending on the goal of the *donor* (the person making the gift). In the example just given, the goal of the donor was to convert non-income producing property to income producing property without paying a high Capital Gains Tax. A wealthy donor may be more concerned about his child paying a high Capital Gains Tax should the child inherit highly appreciated property.

For example, suppose you bought acreage in Georgia that appreciated significantly over the years and is now worth one million dollars. You have been putting off selling the property because of the Capital Gains Tax. But it has been a burden to you. It produces no income and because the property continues to appreciate, each year you are paying more and more in property taxes. You did not mind the sacrifice because you figured that your son would inherit the property at a step-up in basis. But now with the new tax law, by the time you die, the property may be worth three million dollars. He is only allowed a 1.3 million dollar step up in basis, so your son may need to pay a significant Capital Gains Tax when he sells the property.

Setting up a Charitable Remainder Annuity Trust solves the problem of the Capital Gains Tax. The land is transferred to the Charitable Trust. Charities pay no tax, so the Trustee can sell the land and the full market value of the property will be available for investment.

The Trust could be set up with you receiving an income for life, and your son receiving the annuity after your death. The only problem with this arrangement is that your son is significantly younger than you are. There may not be much left to benefit the charity if they must wait for both of you to die. The solution is to have the annuity based on your life only and then use part of the income that you receive to purchase a three million dollar insurance policy on your life with your son as beneficiary. The three million dollars is the estimated value of the land that your son would have inherited at your death. But with this arrangement he will inherit the insurance proceeds free of any Capital Gains Tax.

The astute reader (and probably one with an accounting background) will say "Aha, you may have avoided the Capital Gains Tax, but the Estate Tax Exclusion value does not increase to 3.5 million dollars until the year 2009. The three million dollar life insurance policy counts as part of your taxable Estate, so if you die before 2009, your son will pay an Estate Tax! "

And of course our clever imaginary attorney has a solution in the form of an Irrevocable Insurance Trust. You can set up an Irrevocable Trust so that the Trust owns the insurance policy and not you. The insurance policy is not included in your taxable Estate, so your son pays no Estate Tax. See the end of Chapter 6 for an explanation of how the Irrevocable Insurance Trust works.

As with any Estate Plan you need to consider the downside, and the Charitable Remainder Annuity Trust is no exception.

⊠ ATTORNEY FEES

It may cost significant attorney fees to set up the Trust. Some charities may offer to have their attorney prepare the Trust at no cost to you, or perhaps they offer a "standard" Trust document that their attorney prepared. But using the charity's Trust document represents a conflict of interest. Their Trust was prepared by an attorney for the greatest benefit to his client (that's the charity, not you).

It is important that you employ your own attorney to represent you. He knows the extent of your Estate and he understands what you wish to accomplish.

⊠   THE COMPLEXITY OF THE PLAN

A Charitable Remainder Annuity Trust is a sophisticated Estate Plan designed to benefit the well-to-do donor and an IRS approved charity. There are any number of ways to set up the plan. It is important to have an attorney who will take the time to explore different plans until you determine the best plan for you.

⊠   THE TRUST IS IRREVOCABLE

Once established, the Trust is not revocable, so it is important that you understand all of the aspects of the Trust. In particular, you need to know how much it will cost in attorney's fees to set up the Trust; and how much income you will receive, and over what period of time. The income you receive as an annuitant is taxable to you. You need to consider that while taxes change over the years, the terms of the Trust cannot be changed. It is important that your attorney, accountant or financial planner give you some idea of what you might expect in terms of future income tax payments.

Although future income tax payments may be a question mark, the power of the Charitable Remainder Trust is the tax benefit to the donor at the time the Trust is set up.

☑   NO CAPITAL GAINS TAX

Had you sold the property and invested the money yourself, you would have paid a Capital Gains Tax and that tax could have been substantial, depending on the tax rate in effect at the time of the transfer. By gifting the property the full value of the land can be used to produce investment income.

☑   NO PROPERTY TAX

Once your property is transferred into the Trust, you will no longer need to pay annual property taxes.

☑   NO GIFT TAX

The property you transfer into the Trust is a gift to a charity and as such is not included in the sum total of taxable gifts that you give during your lifetime.

☑   INCOME TAX DEDUCTION

Because you are making a charitable donation, you should be able to take a charitable deduction on your income tax in the year of the donation.

There are other "perks" in addition to the tax benefits:

☑   NO PROBATE EXPENSE

It might take an expensive and time consuming Probate procedure to transfer the property to a beneficiary upon your death. By transferring the property to the Trust during your lifetime, you avoid the need for a Probate procedure to transfer the property after your death.

☑   GIVE WHEN NEEDED INSTEAD OF LATER

A Charitable Remainder Annuity Trust can be set up in any number of different ways to accommodate your Estate Plan. For example, if you are not in need of a present income, but expect that you will spend significant sums on your child's education, you can set up a 20 year annuity with your child as the annuitant. This will get the child through college and probably be a great help should the child decide to start a family. Why have the child inherit property in later, high earning years rather than in the early, high expense/low income years?

☑ CREDITOR PROTECTION

If you keep the land and are sued, you could lose it to pay your creditors. If a beneficiary inherits the land, it could be lost to his/her creditors. But once the property is transferred to the Trust, the gift is made. Neither your creditors nor your beneficiary's creditors can gain access to the Trust funds. The most a creditor can do is seek payment from the money that is received as an income.

☑ GOOD DEED

If you are concerned that your son will be tagged with a Capital Gains Tax once you die, it means that your property has appreciated more than 1.3 million dollars, and you are fortunate indeed. By setting up a Charitable Trust, you are making a donation to the charity of your choice. You are sharing your good fortune with others. You can consider this as "giving back" to the community, or just plain doing a good deed.

BECOME A PHILANTHROPIST

Instead of giving the property to an established charity, you can become a philanthropist and set up your own Charitable foundation. The foundation can be in the form of an IRS approved Charitable Trust. You can be the Trustee of the Charitable Trust and your child the Successor Trustee. The Trust can be set up according to your specific charitable purposes. You can use the Trust to benefit a single cause or several worthy projects. This can be an exciting adventure for those with ample resources and a community spirit.

An Estate Plan For Your Person

The law makes a distinction between your property (what you own) and your person (your body). We have been discussing how to set up an Estate Plan for your property with the goal of maximum control over your Estate during your lifetime, and minimum cost and hassle to your heirs once you die. An Estate Plan for your body is just as important as an Estate Plan for your property. The goals are much the same. Maximum control over your body during your lifetime. Minimum cost and hassle to your family for your final disposition.

You may think it strange to speak of planning for maximum control of your body during your lifetime. After all, it's your body. Who else but you has any right to control what you do with your body? That may be true so long as you have capacity, but should you become seriously ill, you may be unable to express your wishes about the care you wish to receive. If you do not have an Estate Plan in place for your person, your next of kin, or maybe the state of Georgia may make health decisions for you.

The same applies to the final disposition of your body. If you don't make burial and funeral arrangements, then someone will need to make these decisions for you.

As this chapter will show, it is relatively simple and inexpensive to set up an Estate Plan for your Person.

People with a large family often arrange for a family burial site. Over the years deceased family members come to occupy a space in that site, but others may have been buried elsewhere. Surviving family members often lose track of the number of spaces left. If this is the case with your family, you need to take inventory of the number of spaces available and who in the family expects to use those spaces.

Let the cemetery know if there is a change in the expected occupant of the burial site. The cemetery company can charge up to $50 to transfer burial rights from one person to another, but only if the right to charge for the transfer was disclosed to you, in writing, when you purchased the burial site (OCG 10-14-17(d)(2)).

In these days of ever increasing life expectancy, it is important to keep in touch with the cemetery and let them know whenever you change your address. If the site is not used and the cemetery is unable to locate you, after 75 years the cemetery can take legal steps to have the site declared as being abandoned and to sever your rights as the owner of the burial site (OCG 44-5-211).

OUT OF STATE BURIAL SITE

It may be that the family burial site is not in the state of Georgia. In such case, it is important to consider the cost of transporting the body from Georgia to the out-of-state cemetery. That cost can be substantial, in some cases doubling the cost of the burial. If there is no emotional attachment to the out-of-state burial site, you may want to consider assigning the burial site to a family member who lives closer to the site and making your own burial arrangements here in Georgia.

It is important to make your own burial arrangements. Even if it is not important to you where you are buried, it may be very important to your family. That is often the case in second marriages. If you have children from a first marriage, they may want their parents to be "reunited in death."

Your current spouse may not take kindly to having you buried with your former spouse. This might result in hard feelings, if not an out-and-out battle.

The same problem can arise with those in a gay relationship. The decedent's family might not have acknowledged the relationship. The family might decide to have the decedent buried in the family plot and exclude the gay partner from participating in the burial arrangements.

You can head off disputes about your final resting place, by making your own burial arrangements. If you do not do so, Georgia Courts have ruled that your surviving spouse has authority to provide for your final disposition. If you are not survived by a spouse, your next of kin (adult child, parent, sibling, etc.) will make such provision (*Welch v. Welch*, 269 Ga. 742, 505 S.E. 2d 470 (1998), OCG 43-18-1(16)).

Increasingly people are opting for cremation. The reasons for choosing cremation are varied, but for many, it is a matter of finances. The cost of cremation is approximately one-sixth that of an ordinary funeral and burial. A major saving is the cost of the casket. A casket is not necessary for the cremation. An alternate container of fiberboard or similar materials, can be used to transport the body. Embalming is not necessary either, unless there is to be a funeral with a viewing. Federal law prohibits a funeral director from saying that a casket or embalming is necessary for a direct (immediate) cremation (16 Code of Federal Regulations ("CFR") 453.3 (b)(1)(ii)).

For those who are considering cremation, there are a few things to consider.

THE PACEMAKER

Cremating a body with a pacemaker or any radiation producing device can cause damage to the cremation chamber and/or to the person performing the cremation. If you have such an electronic aid, it will need to be removed prior to the cremation. You might check with the cremation service to determine the cost of having the pacemaker removed.

A pacemaker can be donated for use in animals with a medical need for the service. If you are interested in making such donation, you can ask your local veterinarian to refer you to an animal clinic that performs the procedure, and then arrange to have it removed prior to your burial or cremation.

THE OVERWEIGHT

Cremation may not be an option for those who weigh more than 300 pounds. Many cremation services do not have the facilities to handle a large body. If you weigh more than 300 pounds, you need to check with your local cremation service to determine whether this will be a problem.

WHAT TO DO WITH THE ASHES

In addition to planning for the procedure, you need to give your family some guidance as to where to place the ashes. Some cemeteries allow an urn containing the cremated remains of a family member to be placed in an occupied family plot. Similarly, some cemeteries will allow the cremated remains to be placed in the space in a mausoleum that is currently occupied by a member of the decedent's family. If you intend to be cremated and all your family spaces are occupied you may want to call the cemetery and ask them to explain their policy as it relates to the burial of urns in occupied sites.

If burial in the family site is not an option, you will need to arrange for a separate burial space. Many cemeteries have a separate building called a *columbarium*, which is especially designed to store urns. You can purchase a storage place for the urn in the same manner as the purchase of a burial space in a cemetery.

BURIAL AT SEA

If you wish a family member to scatter your ashes at sea, he will need to comply with Georgia law. The law requires that the burial be completed within 50 days from the date of the cremation and at a point no closer than three miles from the nearest shoreline. The person who conducts the burial at sea needs to file a record of the burial with the Registrar in the county nearest the point where the ashes were scattered (OCG 31-21-4).

THE MILITARY BURIAL

If you are an honorably discharged veteran or the spouse of such veteran, you have the right to be buried in a Veterans National Cemetery. If your Veteran spouse was buried in a Veterans National Cemetery, you have the right to be buried in that same grave site unless soil conditions require a separate burial site.

You can get information about burial at a Veterans National Cemetery by calling the Veteran's Administration at (800) 827-1000, or visiting their Web site.

 VA CEMETERY WEB SITE
http://www.cem.va.gov

The Web site has information on the following topics:
  - ➢ National and Military Cemeteries
  - ➢ Burial, Headstones and Markers
  - ➢ State Cemetery Grants Program

You cannot reserve a grave site in advance, so your family will need to make arrangements and establish your eligibility to be buried in a Veterans National Cemetery. At that time, they will need to provide the following information:
  - ➢ your rank, serial, social security and VA claim numbers
  - ➢ the branch of service in which you served; the date and place of your entry into and separation from the service
  - ➢ a copy of your official military discharge document bearing an official seal or a DD 214 form.

If you wish to be buried in a national cemetery, you need to make all of these items readily accessible to your family.

THE PRENEED FUNERAL CONTRACT

If you are financially able, in addition to arranging a burial space, consider purchasing a Preneed Funeral Contract. It will be easier on your family emotionally and financially if you make your own funeral arrangements. Federal law requires that you receive a general price list at the beginning of any discussion for the purchase of funeral services (16 CFR 453.2).

Once you decide upon a plan, the seller should give you a contract that states the prices charged for *services* (embalming, viewing, transportation, etc.) and *merchandise purchased* (casket, urn, acknowledgment cards, register books, clothing, etc.) and *cash advance items*, i.e., things paid for by the funeral director and then reimbursed back to him. This includes paying for death certificates, arranging to have the obituary printed, payment for religious services, etc. (16 CFR 453.5, OCG 10-14-19).

Even though the seller gives you a "standard" contract that is prepared according to Georgia law, it does not mean that it cannot be changed. If you are not satisfied with the way a certain section of the contract reads, attach an addendum to the contract that explains, in plain English, your understanding of that passage. If you are concerned about something that is not mentioned in the contract, insist the contract be amended to include that item.

In particular, check to see whether the contract answers the following questions.

Does the contract cover all costs?

The contract should contain an itemized list stating exactly what goods and services are included in the sales price. Your contract may include an allowance towards cash advance items such as the printing of the obituary or payment to the clergy, or your contract may provide that payment be made at the time of the funeral. Your contract should state that the amount charged by the funeral director for a cash advance item be no more than the amount paid by the director for that item.

Is the price guaranteed?

Some Preneed Funeral Plans have a fixed price for the goods and services you choose, meaning that the funeral director will provide the goods and services at the same price as agreed at the time of the contract. It is important that your contract state that the person or company who is selling you the Funeral Plan is the same person or company who will actually provide those goods and services. If not, you need to have the provider of the goods and services sign the contract saying that he agrees to be bound by the terms of your agreement. If the seller says that it is not necessary for the provider to sign your contract because he and the provider have a separate written agreement, then have that agreement attached to your contract.

You might opt for a Preneed Funeral Contract that is not a fixed price; meaning that the company can charge additional monies for the plan that you have chosen upon your death. In these days of an ever increasing life expectancy, it is important that such a contract clearly state how the price will be determined when the contract is finally put into effect.

How are your contract funds protected?

You can fund your Preneed Funeral Plan by purchasing a life insurance policy. Georgia law prohibits the funeral director from selling a life insurance policy to you to pay for your plan, however, you can purchase a life insurance policy from an insurance company, and assign the proceeds of the policy to the funeral establishment as payment for the plan (OCG 33-1-10, 33-1-12). It is important to carefully review the terms of the insurance policy, especially as it relates to your right to cancel the policy and receive a refund, and your right to cancel the Preneed contract and assign the proceeds to another company or person.

ESCROW ACCOUNT

You may decide to pay cash for your Preneed Funeral Plan. Georgia law requires that the funeral director place the funds in an escrow account within 30 days following the month in which the payment is made (OCG 10-14-7)(b)). You may want to have your contract require the deposit be made within a shorter period of time. You may also want your contract to require that you receive proof of deposit within that period of time and that you be notified in the event that the location of the escrow account is changed for whatever reason.

It is also important that the contract state what percentage of your funds will be deposited to the escrow account. Georgia law requires that the amount deposited be no less than 110% of the wholesale price of the item, but in the case of a casket, this may be only 35% of the amount you paid under your contract. Monies in the escrow account belong to you during your lifetime. The escrow agent will pay the funds in the account to the funeral firm upon your death.

But there are downsides to such plan:

INTEREST IS INCOME TO YOU

Because you own the account, interest on that account will be included as taxable income to you.

SERVICE FEE

The bank may charge a service fee for your account. That amount is deducted from your account.

Can you cancel the contract?

Your contract needs to clearly state under what terms and conditions you cancel the contract. Many contracts allow you to cancel the contract , provided the company keeps a certain percentage of the funds. If you are paying on an installment plan, you need to know how much of the monies you paid will be returned to you in the event that you default on making payment.

Is the funeral firm reputable?

All these protections don't do much good if you are not dealing with a reputable company. It is important to take the time to check up on whoever is selling you the contract. In Georgia, anyone who offers Preneed contracts to the public must be licensed to do so (OCG 10-14-4). You can check to see if the seller is licensed by calling the Georgia Secretary of State. Under Georgia law your Preneed Funeral Contract should contain the telephone number of the Secretary of State (OCG 10-14-18(b)(4)). If you want to check before signing a contract, you can call the State Examining Board at (478) 207-1460. You may want to ask how long the firm has been in business and whether any complaints have been filed against them.

Suppose you die in another state or country?

Your contract should spell out what provision will be made in the event that you move to another state or die in another state or country. Many funeral firms are part of a national funeral service corporation with funeral firms located throughout the United States. You may be able to have the contract provide that there will be no additional charge if the contract is performed by one of the funeral firms owned by the parent company.

Can the plan be changed after your death?

It may happen that your heirs need to cancel the plan after your death because:

➢   your body is missing or cannot be recovered, or

➢   you were buried by another facility because no one knew that you had a Preneed contract, or

➢   you died in another country and were buried there.

Your contract should address these potential problems, and spell out how much money will be refunded and who is to receive the refund.

You may also want to specify whether your heirs have the right to alter your funeral plans. In the absence of such a provision in the contract, funeral firms usually allow the family to arrange for a more expensive plan, provided they agree to pay the difference.

You may wonder why anyone would think of changing the decedent's funeral plan, but consider that in today's market, it is not uncommon for a Preneed Funeral Plan to cost several thousand dollars. A top end funeral complete with solid bronze casket can cost upwards of $30,000. Some heirs might be motivated to save money by changing the plan to one of a lesser value.

That was the case with Lester. His mother, Mona, was a difficult woman with a personality that can only be described as "sour." Her husband deserted her after four years of marriage leaving her to raise Lester by herself. Once Lester was grown, Mona made it clear to him that she had done her job and now he was on his own. Lester could have used some help. He married and had three children. One of his children suffered with asthma and it was a constant struggle to keep up with the medical bills.

Mona believed in being good to herself. She did not intend to, nor did she, leave much money when she died. She knew that Lester would not be able to afford a "proper" burial for her, so she purchased a funeral plan and paid close to $18,000 for it. She was pleased when the funeral director told her that the monies would be kept safely in a Trust account until the time they were needed.

Lester was not familiar with Georgia law, so when his mother died he asked an attorney at the Legal Service office to determine whether the Preneed contract was revocable.

It was.

You know the ending to this story.

The reader may be thinking "Revocable, irrevocable. All this contract stuff is giving me a headache. Why can't I just set aside some money and let my kids figure it out?"

The problem with that approach is that the cost of your final illness may leave you with little or no funds for your burial. To avoid the problem, you could purchase a life insurance policy to fund your funeral and burial, naming a trusted family member as the beneficiary of the policy.

It is important that the person who is to receive the insurance proceeds clearly understands why he is named as beneficiary. It is equally important that the beneficiary agree to use the monies for the intended purpose.

It isn't so much that a family member is not trustworthy as it is that they may not understand what you intended — especially in those cases where other funds are available to pay for the funeral. Too often insurance funds are left to a child who refuses to contribute to the cost of the funeral saying "Dad wanted me to have this money. That's why he left it to me."

To avoid a misunderstanding, put it in writing. It need not be a formal contract. It could be something as simple as a letter to the insurance beneficiary, with copies to your next of kin. See the next page for an example of such letter.

Dear Paul,

I purchased a $20,000 insurance policy today naming you as beneficiary of the policy.

As we discussed this money is to be used to pay for the following:
- *my funeral, grave site and headstone*
- *perpetual care for my grave*
- *airfare for each of my grandchildren to attend the funeral*
- *dinner for the family after the wake*
- *lunch for the family after the funeral*

If there is any money left over, please accept it as my thanks for all the effort spent on my behalf.
Love,
  Dad

P.S. I am sending a copy of this letter to your sister so that she will know that all arrangements have been made.

ANATOMICAL GIFT

If you want to make an anatomical gift to take effect upon your death, you can make the gift as part of your Will; but it may be some time before your Will is located. The better route is to make the donation by a separate writing. You can complete an organ donor card when you apply for your Georgia driver's license or Georgia Photo Identification Card. If you do not want the fact that you are an organ donor indicated on your driver's license or Photo ID, you can sign a HEALTH CARE POWER OF ATTORNEY and appoint a trusted friend or family member to carry out your wishes. We will discuss how to prepare a Health Care Power of Attorney later in this chapter.

If you do not sign a donor card, Georgia statute gives an order of priority for those who can give permission to make an anatomical gift on your behalf:

1st your spouse
2nd an adult son or daughter
3rd either parent
4th an adult brother or sister
5th your grandparent
6th your Court appointed Guardian (if any)
7th anyone authorized to dispose of the body

An effort must be made to contact the person with highest priority. For example, if your sister agrees to the donation (4th in priority) and you have adult children (2nd in priority), your children need to be made aware of the gift. If a child objects, no gift can be made. Similarly, the statute prohibits the gift if you ever expressed your opposition to making a donation (OCG 44-5-143, 44-5-145).

GIFT FOR EDUCATION AND RESEARCH

There is no age limit on organ and tissue donations, however doctors will probably not consider your body suitable for transplantation if you are of advanced age and in poor health. You can still donate your body to a school of medicine or dentistry for education and research. You can call or write to the following schools for information about making a donation:

Mercer University
School of Medicine
1550 College St., Box 153
Macon, GA 31206
Telephone (478) 301-4074

Emory Body Donor Program
P.O. Drawer AR
Atlanta, GA   30322-0001
Telephone (404) 727-6242

Medical College of Georgia in Augusta
1120 15th Street, CB 2915
Augusta, GA   30912-9974
Telephone (706) 721-3731

Schools want to be assured that the donation is being made by the person himself, rather than his family, so they ask donors to preregister with the school at least 90 days prior to the death. Policies regarding transportation of the body vary school to school. Mercer University will pay for the transportation, provided the body is within 50 miles of Macon. Emory does not pay for transportation, so the family must arrange for delivery. The Medical College of Georgia in Augusta will provide transportation from any where in Georgia for donors who are preregistered. You can download a registration form from the Medical College of Georgia Web site. http://www.mcg.edu/

There could be a substantial transportation fee should you die far from the school, so you need to give your family instructions about what to do in such csse. Similarly, schools will not accept a body weighing over 300 pounds or one who died from a contagious disease or crushing injury, so you need to make alternate provision for such events.

AUTOPSIES

An autopsy is one of those things that most of us do not think about; reasoning that if it is needed, it will be carried out and, being dead, you will have no choice in the matter. But there are many times when an autopsy is optional. Sometimes a doctor is not sure of the cause of death, and asks the family to allow an autopsy. It is often in the family's best interest to consent to the autopsy. The examination might reveal a genetic disorder, that could be treated if it later appears in another family member. Death from a car "accident" could have been a heart attack at the wheel. Perhaps the patient who died suddenly in a hospital was misdiagnosed. The nursing home resident could have died from negligence and not old age. Even if none of these are found, knowing the cause of death with certainty is better than not knowing.

Whoever takes custody of the body for burial (spouse, parent, sibling, next of kin) may give permission for the examination. If none of these are available, a friend or whoever is responsible to arrange the burial may authorize the autopsy (OCG 45-16-28).

The person giving authorization for an optional autopsy must agree to pay for the autopsy because the cost is not covered under most health insurance plans. An autopsy can cost anywhere from several hundred to several thousand dollars. Still another reason family members hesitate to allow the procedure is that they do not know how the decedent would have felt about the examination.

If you have strong feelings one way or another, let your family know how you feel about an optional autopsy.

Of course, there are problems with just telling someone how you feel about your burial arrangements, autopsies, and anatomical gifts:

YOU TELL THE WRONG PERSON
You may tell someone who does not have authority to carry out your wishes. That was the case with James. When his wife died, he moved to a retirement community where he lived for several years until his death. James had two sons who lived in different states. Although he loved his sons, he had difficulty talking to either of them about serious matters. It was easier for him to talk with his friends in the retirement community. They often spoke about dying and how they felt about different burial arrangements. James would reminisce about his youth and growing up in a farming community in the plains state of Kansas. "I was happy and free. Out there you had room to breathe. It would be nice to be buried there — peaceful and spacious."

When he died, his friends told his sons about their father's desire to be buried in Kansas. They met the suggestion with scepticism and pragmatism:

"Dad didn't say anything like that to me."

"It would cost us double, if we had to arrange for burial in another state. I'm sure he didn't have that kind of expense in mind."

THE PERSON DOES NOT CARRY OUT YOUR WISHES
Sometimes the person you tell about the disposition of your body may not understand what you said or perhaps they hear only what they want to hear. Whether they follow your burial instructions or authorize an anatomical gift or an autopsy may depend more about what costs are involved, and their own feelings, rather than what you may have wanted.

Even if you tell someone and trust that person to carry out your wishes, it could be that the person you confide in cannot carry out your instructions. For example, if you tell your spouse what arrangements to make, he/she may become incapacitated or die before you do; or perhaps you both die together in a natural disaster or in a plane crash.

WHO WANTS TO TALK ABOUT IT?

For many people the main problem with telling someone what to do when you die is talking about your death. It may be an uncomfortable, if not unpleasant, subject for you to bring up, and for your family to discuss. If this is the case, then consider putting the information in writing and give the instructions to the person who will have the job of carrying out your wishes.

Making provision for the disposition of your body is important, but it is more important to make sure that you are in control of the health care you receive should you become seriously ill. This is not a problem when you are well enough to make your own medical decisions; however it could happen that you are too ill to let people know what you want.

The solution to the problem is appoint someone to serve as your HEALTH CARE AGENT. You can give your Agent instructions about medical treatment that you do, or do not, want to receive. You can give your Agent authority to see that your instructions are followed.

You can legally appoint someone to carry out your wishes relating to the care of your person, by signing a document called a *Durable Power of Attorney For Health Care.* The word "durable" means that the document is effective if you are incapacitated and unable to speak for yourself. You can have your attorney prepare a Health Care Power of Attorney to meet your special needs or you can prepare your own Power of Attorney by using the form provided in Georgia statute (OCG 31-36-10). You can download the form from the Georgia Statute Web site.

http://www.legis.state.ga.us

The person you appoint as your *Health Care Agent* under the Durable Power of Attorney will be able to make your medical decisions in the event that you are too ill to do so yourself. He will also have full authority over the final disposition of your body, including authority to order an autopsy or make an anatomical gift (OCG 31-36-4).

You can sign a *Living Will* giving directions about whether you do (or do not) want life-sustaining or death-delaying treatment in the event that you are dying and there is no hope for your recovery. There is a statutory form of Living Will included in Georgia statute (OCG 31-32-3). You can include the Living Will as part of your Durable Power of Attorney For Health Care and give your Health Care Agent authority to see to it that the instructions you give relating to such treatment, are followed.

MAKING ANATOMICAL GIFTS
You can make an anatomical gift by signing an organ donor card. You can give your Health Care Agent authority to carry out your wishes. If you do not wish to make an anatomical gift, you can direct your Health Care Agent not to allow the procedure.

USING THE DIRECTIVE TO AUTHORIZE AN AUTOPSY

You can use your Health Care Power of Attorney to authorize an autopsy, or you can withhold your consent for the performance of an optional autopsy, or you can leave the decision in the hands of your Health Care Agent (OCG 45-16-28).

MEDICAL DECISIONS IF NO HEALTH CARE AGENT

If you do not appoint someone to be your Health Care Agent and give that person authority to act in accordance with directions given in your Durable Power of Attorney For Health Care, the person with authority to direct your medical treatment is determined by Georgia Statute.

Under Georgia law, the following persons have priority to make your medical decisions in the event you are too ill to do so yourself:

> 1st your spouse
> 2nd your adult children
> 3rd your parent
> 4th your adult brother or sister
> 5th your grandparent (OCG 31-9-2).

A person with priority must be reasonably available, willing and competent to make medical decisions for you. If not, the next one with priority will make the decision.

If this order of priority is not as you wish, or if there is someone you wish to exclude altogether from making your health care decisions, then it is important to sign a Durable Power of Attorney For Health Care and appoint the person of your choice to act as your Health Care Agent. If not, life decisions made for you, may not be as you would have wished. That was the case with George.

George was a devoted husband and father. His wife came down with Alzheimer's disease. George cared for her at home, but finally it was too much for him and he had to place her in a nursing home. He and his daughters often visited, although she scarcely recognized them.

George met Emily during one of his visits. Her husband also suffered from Alzheimer's and was a resident of the nursing home. George and Emily had much in common. After visiting with their respective spouses, they would go to the local coffee shop. One thing led to another and soon they were an item.

George's daughters were not happy with his "lady friend." They criticized everything about her. From the way she dressed, to her table manners. Emily did not take it personally. She believed the girls were more interested in their expected inheritance, than George's happiness. A second marriage might cut into what they considered to be rightfully theirs.

Not that George and Emily planned to wed. They both loved their respective spouses and had no intention of trying to obtain a divorce. They just enjoyed each other's company. Caring for their respective spouses , they learned to take it one day at a time. That philosophy carried over into their relationship. They were both content to enjoy social outings with each other — dinner, movies, playing golf, and so on.

Both were happier than they had been in years. But that happiness was short-lived. George suffered a stroke while driving a car. He was seriously injured and lapsed into a coma. The prognosis was not encouraging. The doctors said George would die unless they put him on a ventilator and inserted a feeding tube. Even with these life support systems, they were not promising that he would survive.

Emily pleaded to keep him alive. "Let's try everything. If he doesn't improve, we can always discontinue the life support systems later."

George's daughters did not see it that way. "Why torture him with needles and tubes. Let him pass on peacefully."

George never signed a Living Will, so no one knew how he felt about life support systems. He never appointed anyone to be his Health Care Agent to make his medical decisions now that he was unable to do so himself. In the absence of a Durable Power of Attorney For Health Care, the doctors followed Georgia law. George's spouse had priority to direct his treatment however because she was unable to do so, his daughters had the right to make medical decisions for their father.

Emily had no priority at all.

George died.

A Health Care Estate Plan 9

We discussed an Estate Plan as it relates to the distribution or management of your Estate once you are deceased. In this age of extended life expectancy, a more pressing concern is how to manage and preserve your Estate in the event of a debilitating illness. As life expectancy increases, so does the percentage of the population who suffer incapacitating strokes, Alzheimer's disease or Parkinson's disease. It is estimated that more than half of the population who are 85 or older, have some degree of dementia. Your best Estate Plan could be sabotaged by a lengthy illness. In this chapter we will explore ways to pay for the health care that you may require as you age.

In addition to paying for your health care, you need to consider who will care for your finances and everyday physical needs in the event that you are too ill to do so yourself. A *Health Care Estate Plan* is a plan designed to care for your person and property in the event of an incapacitating illness. In the last chapter, we discussed how you can appoint a Health Care Agent to care for your person in the event of your incapacity.

But there is still the problem of who will care for your property. In this chapter we will discuss how you can appoint someone to care for your property and manage your finances in the event of your incapacity.

The optimum way to provide for the care of your property in the event of your incapacity is to set up a Trust appointing a Successor Trustee to care for your property according to the directions given in your Trust. You can be Trustee of the funds while you have capacity. Should you become incapacitated, then the person you name as Successor Trustee will take over. But if you do not have sufficient assets to justify the cost of employing an attorney to draft a Trust, then there are other strategies that you can use to solve the problem.

THE JOINT ACCOUNT
You can set up a joint checking account so that a trusted family member can write checks on the account. Of course there are all the inherent problems of a joint account that we discussed in Chapter 2. You can avoid many of those problems by limiting the amount of money that can be accessed by the family member. For example, you can arrange your finances so that all of your bills are paid from a single checking account and your family member can access that account, only.

THE AGENCY ACCOUNT
If you set up a joint account, your family member will own whatever is in the account should you die. If this is not as you wish, you can instruct the bank that this is an *Agency* or *Convenience* account and that, in the event of your death, the family member may no longer access your account. But ultimately the family member must be trustworthy because the bank is under no duty to stop your family member from writing checks on your account until the bank learns of your death. Even with that knowledge, the bank can, for ten days, continue to pay checks drawn on or before the death, unless someone who has an interest in your account orders them to immediately stop payment (OCG 11-4-405, 7-1-816).

The joint or convenience account solves the problem of how to pay your bills in the event you are temporarily ill. It does not solve the problem of how to manage your business affairs in the event of an extended illness. For example, suppose you have a stroke and can no longer be cared for at home. Should it be necessary for you to sell your home and move to an assisted living facility, no one will have the authority to sell the house for you. In such case, your friends or family members may need to ask the Court to appoint a Conservator to manage your finances, and if you did not appoint a Health Care Agent, a Guardian to make your medical decisions and care for your person.

Before doing so, the Court will need to be convinced that you are unable to care for your person and/or property. He will set a time for a hearing on the matter and have an officer of the Court hand deliver a notice to you explaining the nature of the court proceeding. It will give the time and place of the hearing and advise you of your right to attend the hearing and be represented by an attorney of your choice. Notice of the proceeding will be sent to your spouse and children. If you have no adult children, the Court will send notice to at least two adults in the following order of priority:

        1st your lineal descendants
        2nd your parents and siblings
        3rd your friends

If you do not employ an attorney, the Court will appoint one for you. The Court will order that you be examined by a physician, psychologist, or licensed clinical social worker, who will submit an evaluation report to the Court (OCG 29-4-11, 29-5-11, 29-9-15).

Determining whether you have capacity to take care of yourself can be an embarrassing, and demeaning experience, if you are sufficiently aware of the proceedings. If the Court decides that you are incapacitated, he will appoint a Conservator to care for your property and/or a Guardian to care for your person.

If a Guardian of your person is appointed, he will see to your health care. Each year, he will need to prepare and file a Personal Status Report regarding your well-being (OCG 29-4-22). If a Conservator for your property is appointed he will take possession of your assets and file an inventory with the Court. The Court will order your Conservator to obtain a bond for the protection of your assets. Each year the Conservator must account to the Court for monies spent. He may need to employ an accountant to help prepare the inventory and annual accounting. All of these expenses are a proper charge to your Estate (OCG 29-5-30, 29-5-40, 29-5-51).

The Conservator is entitled to be paid for his services. The amount set by Georgia law is 2 1/2% on all sums of money received as part of the conservatorship Estate each year, plus 0.5% of the market value of property held in the Estate and 10% commission of the amount of interest earned on conservatorship property. If there is some unusual problem such as a law suit, the Conservator can ask the Court for additional compensation (OCG 29-5-50, 29-2-52). The Conservator will need to employ an attorney to establish the conservatorship to see that reports to the Court are properly and timely filed. Monies paid to the attorney for the Conservator are a proper charge to your Estate. There is no statutory amount, however the rate approved by the Court is comparable to fees paid to the attorney of other fiduciaries such as a Trustee or Personal Representative (OCG 29-9-15).

Court filing fees, the competency examination fee, the cost of a bond, accounting fees, the Guardian/Conservator's fee, your attorney's fee and the Guardian/Conservator's attorney fees, all are paid from your Estate (that's your money!)

A guardianship and/or conservatorship is expensive to set up and maintain. Curious that so many people worry about how to avoid Probate, when the greater concern should be how to avoid a guardianship and conservatorship. It is not all that hard to arrange your finances so that no Probate is necessary. The cost to transfer your property to your beneficiaries should be minimal.

Even with a full Probate procedure, whatever it costs to Probate your Estate is a one-time expense. And Probate is a one-time procedure. Once monies are distributed to your beneficiaries, it is over. Not so if you become incapacitated. It can cost thousands of dollars to set up the guardianship/conservatorship; and more money to care for you and your property each year. And this expense goes on, year after year, until you are returned to capacity, or die.

As with Probate it is not all that hard to avoid these unnecessary charges to your Estate. To avoid the need for a Guardian of your person, you can appoint a Health Care Agent to make your medical decisions should you be too ill to do so yourself (see Chapter 8).

To avoid the need for a Conservator, you can set up a Trust and appoint a Successor Trustee to care for your property in the event of your incapacity. For those of limited means, the FINANCIAL POWER OF ATTORNEY is the next best Estate plan.

A POWER OF ATTORNEY FOR FINANCES

A *Financial Power of Attorney* is a legal document by which someone (the *Principal*) gives another (his *Agent* or *Attorney-In-Fact*) authority to do certain acts on behalf of the Principal. If you wish to have someone be able to conduct business on your behalf in the event of your physical incapacity, you can make the Power of Attorney *durable* by including the phrase "It is my desire that this power of attorney shall not be affected by my subsequent disability, incapacity, or mental incompetence."

There is a statutory form of a Durable Financial Power of Attorney (OCG 10-6-142) that you can copy at your local law library or you can download it from the Internet.

GEORGIA STATUTE
http://www.legis.state.ga.us

The statutory form enables you to give your Attorney-In-Fact the power to do any of the following:
⇨ make bank or credit union transactions
⇨ pay your bills and taxes
⇨ buy, sell, lease, mortgage, exchange real property on your behalf
⇨ buy, sell, lease, mortgage, exchange any of your personal property
⇨ trade in securities (stocks, bonds, etc.)
⇨ have free access to your safe deposit box
⇨ borrow money on your behalf
⇨ operate your business
⇨ sue or defend a law suit on your behalf
⇨ employ people (attorneys, accountants, doctors, nurses, workers, etc.) on your behalf

Notice that there are many things that your Attorney-In-Fact can do for you personally, such as suing or defending a law suit on your behalf or applying for government benefits. Even if you have a Trust, it is important to appoint someone under a Durable Power of Attorney to do these important, personal, things for you, in the event you can't. Your Trust can only authorize your Successor Trustee to manage property that is placed in your Trust. Your Successor Trustee has no authority over you, personally. But you can give him (or anyone else) that authority by making him your Attorney-In-Fact under a Financial Power of Attorney.

The statutory form enables you to give your Attorney-In-Fact broad powers, however, as we will see in the next chapter, it is important that you give your Attorney-In-Fact specific authority to apply for government benefits on your behalf in the event you are too ill to do so yourself. To be effective the document must state that your Attorney-In-Fact has authority to take whatever steps necessary to qualify you for Medical Assistance, even if that means making gifts or transfers to your family members. The statutory form does not have a section that specifically addresses these issues, so if you are of advanced years, or in poor health, it may be better for you to have your attorney prepare a Financial Power of Attorney to meet your special needs.

GENERAL VS. LIMITED POWER OF ATTORNEY

You can sign a Power of Attorney giving your Attorney-In-Fact broad general powers. With these powers your Attorney-In-Fact can do much the same with your property as you can. If this is of concern to you, instead of giving a General Power of Attorney, you can give a *Limited Power of Attorney* and restrict the things your Attorney-In-Fact can do to just those things authorized in the document.

One power that should be specifically granted in your Power of Attorney, is the power to apply for medical assistance benefits in the event of your incapacity. In the next chapter we will be discussing the many things you can do to qualify for Medicaid. You need to give someone authority to take the necessary steps for you to become eligible for government benefits, in the event you are too ill to do so yourself. Even if you do not wish to give someone control over your finances at this time, you should give someone a Limited Power of Attorney for the purpose of qualifying for Medicaid.

Limited or General, the operative word in any Power of Attorney is POWER. Once your Attorney-In-Fact has authority to act, he essentially steps into your shoes and can do whatever you gave him authority to do. Your primary consideration in choosing an Attorney-In-Fact is trustworthiness. You need to choose someone who will follow your instructions and put the Power of Attorney to the use you intended. You need to choose someone, who, when using your Power of Attorney, will always put your interests ahead of his.

You may be less concerned with trustworthiness than the loss of independence. But the thing to keep in mind is that you still have the power to do all of the things you gave your Attorney-In-Fact authority to do. The only difference is that now, you both have the power to conduct your business transactions.

Of course, shared authority is still less independent than sole authority; so you may hesitate to give someone a Power of Attorney until it is needed. But if you wait until it is needed, you may be too sick to sign the document. There are two simple solutions to this dilemma: keep it in your possession, or make it effective only upon your incapacity.

USING THE POWER OF ATTORNEY

An Attorney-In-Fact under a Power of Attorney cannot operate on behalf of the Principal, unless he has possession of the original Power of Attorney and presents it to whomever he wants to rely on that document. For example, if your Attorney-In-Fact wants to use the Power of Attorney to sell one of your securities, he will need to produce the original document and perhaps sign an *Affidavit* (a written statement sworn to before a Notary Public) saying that the Power of Attorney is still in effect and that you did not revoke that Power of Attorney.

KEEP THE DOCUMENT IN YOUR POSSESSION

Before anyone (a bank, stockbroker, closing agent, etc.) will accept the Power of Attorney they will want to see the original document so that they are assured that your Attorney-In-Fact has authority to transact business on your behalf. If you keep the original document in your possession and do not give anyone a copy, your Attorney-In-Fact will not be able to act for you.

The only problem with this arrangement is that you need to arrange to make the document accessible to your Attorney-In-Fact in the event of your incapacity. If your Attorney-In-Fact is a trusted family member, you can give him the location of the document with instructions to take possession of the Durable Power of Attorney in the event of your incapacity.

THE SPRINGING POWER OF ATTORNEY

A better solution may be to have a "springing" Financial Power of Attorney that is not operational until your family doctor and/or independent physician says that you are incapacitated and unable to manage your financial affairs. Your Attorney-In-Fact can hold the original document, but cannot use it until it "springs to life" when a doctor determines that you are too ill to care for your property (OCG 10-6-141, 10-6-142).

You can create a Springing Durable Power of Attorney by adding the following provision to your document:

> The powers conveyed in this document shall not become effective until the following time or upon the occurrence of the following event or contingency:
>
> _____

The event or contingency could be documentation that you are disabled or incapacitated such as:

> My regularly attending physician and _____ (name of family member) sign an Affidavit stating that I am disabled or incapacitated.

It is relatively simple and inexpensive to head off guardianship/conservatorship. To avoid a guardianship you can appoint a Health Care Agent under a Durable Power of Attorney for Health Care to make your medical care decisions. To avoid conservatorship, you can appoint an Attorney-In-Fact under a Financial Power of Attorney to manage your finances to care for your property in the event of your incapacity. But, despite your best plans, something unusual could happen causing a Court to decide that you need a Guardian and/or Conservator.

For example, suppose you disappear and cannot be found after a diligent search. It might be necessary to have a Court appoint someone to manage your property in your absence. Or perhaps you develop an addiction or a mental illness causing self-destructive behavior. Your friends or family might decide that you are in need of protection and ask a Court to appoint a Guardian to care for you.

Although it may not be possible to avoid all guardianship/conservator procedures, you can have a measure of control over your fate. Georgia statute gives you the right to name the person of your choice to serve as your Guardian and/or Conservator.

You can appoint someone to serve as your Guardian as part of your Durable Power of Attorney For Health Care. You can include a provision in your Financial Power of Attorney giving your Attorney-In-Fact authority to serve as your Conservator, should the need arise (OCG 29-4-3, 29-5-3).

If you do not express your choice of Conservator or Guardian, and two people want one, or both, jobs, Georgia statue establishes an order of priority for the appointment:

1st   your spouse or someone nominated (i.e., named) by your spouse in a signed and witnessed document

2nd   your adult child or someone nominated by your child in a signed and witnessed document

3rd   your parent or someone nominated by your parent in a signed and witnessed document

4th   a Guardian/Conservator appointed for you when you were a minor

5th   a Guardian/Conservator appointed for you in another state

6th   a friend, relative or other individual

7th   the County Guardian (OCG 29-4-3, 29-5-3).

The judge will give preference to those with top priority, however, the choice of Guardian/Conservator is his. In making the selection, he will be guided by your best interests; meaning that he will chose the person he thinks will do the best job in caring for you. However, some people look good on paper, but in fact may be a poor choice. For example, suppose the Court finds that a woman is not capable of handling her finances and is need of a Conservator. If her son and daughter both want the job, the Court will consider their backgrounds and current commitments. If the son is a college graduate with a degree in accounting and the daughter a homemaker with three small children, the judge might think the son a better choice. But the son might not have been his mother's choice because of the many times she bailed him out of debt.

Again, it is a matter of planning ahead, and being in charge of your own destiny, rather than leaving the choice for a judge to decide.

The good news: You are going to live longer.

The bad news: It's going to cost you.

Scientists are doing a great job of prolonging life, but unless they find Ponce De Leon's fountain, the general population will continue to age. Along with age comes infirmities. Eyes fail. Hearing diminishes. Mobility declines. Digestive systems either speed up or slow down, all to the discomfort of the unhappy occupant of the body. It's all part of the "golden" years. The pharmacology industry is well motivated to produce drugs that manage the ills associated with aging. Their research has led to a wealth of pharmaceutic products that do not cure, but do allow people to live in relative comfort into advanced age. The only problem is the cost of these drugs. Medicare covers the treatment of life-threatening brushes with heart disease, stroke, cancer and diabetes; but, as of this writing, Medicare does not pay for maintenance medication that is often necessary once the condition is stabilized.

Medicare is also limited in long term nursing care coverage. It does not pay for extended nursing care. The federal government now offers the Original Medicare Plan and Medicare Advantage Plans. If you remain with the Original Medicare Plan you do not pay for the first 20 days of skilled nursing care. You pay up to $109.50** per day for days 21 through 100. If you do not have Medicare Supplemental Insurance coverage, it will cost you up to $8,760 for the next 80 days. After 100 days, you are on your own. A nursing home stay of one or two years can wipe out the life savings of most working people. Once savings are gone, the government provides care in the form of Medicaid coverage.

**This is the value for the year 2005. The federal government adjusts the amount each year.

If you have no assets to speak of, and a relatively low income, the cost of long-term nursing care is the least of your worries. Medicaid is available to take care of your medical and nursing care needs. And no need to worry if you are wealthy. You have enough money to pay for any care that you might need. The rest of us need to think about ways to provide for long-term health care.

For those concerned about the loss of life savings because of illness, there is supplemental and/or long-term health care insurance. There are many different insurance plans available. You can call the National Association of Insurance Commissioners at (816) 842-3600 and they will forward to you, free of charge, the publication:

A SHOPPER'S GUIDE TO LONG TERM CARE INSURANCE

If you have a specific question, you can call the CONSUMERS INSURANCE ADVOCATE at (404) 463-1010, or you can visit their Web site.

CONSUMERS INSURANCE ADVOCATE
http://www.insuranceadvocate.org

LONG TERM INSURANCE FOR FEDERAL EMPLOYEES

The Long Term Care Security Act (Public Law 106-265) was passed by Congress to take effect in October, 2002. The law is designed to make long term care insurance available to federal and postal employees, members of the uniformed services, civilian and military retirees, and their qualified relatives. You can call the Office of Personnel Management at (800) 582-3337 for information about the program or visit their Web site.

OFFICE OF PERSONNEL MANAGEMENT
http://www.opm.gov/insure/ltc

The National Association Of Retired Federal Employees ("NARFE") has been actively involved in developing this legislation. You can get information about the program at the NARFE office in Alexandria, Virginia at (703) 838-7780 or from their Web site.

 NATIONAL ASSOC. OF RETIRED FEDERAL EMPLOYEES
http://www.narfe.org

THE PROBLEM OF COST AND ELIGIBILITY

Long term care insurance sounds like the perfect solution, until you start examining the cost. The cost isn't too bad if you are comparatively young, say in your 50s. But can you imagine paying that premium each month until you are in your 80s and never needing nursing care?

Many decide to wait till they are old and going downhill. But that just brings other problems. The older you are, the greater the cost of insurance. And there is the risk that you will be refused coverage because of a "pre-existing" condition, i.e., the insurance company may consider you to be too great a risk for them to insure.

Different insurance companies have come up with insurance plans that may provide a solution for the person who is relatively young and in good health. Some companies offer long-term care insurance that is paid-up within a fixed period of time. Once payments are made for a certain number of years, the person is insured for long-term care without further payment. Other companies combine long-term care insurance with a life insurance policy. They offer long-term care insurance that converts to a life insurance policy, if it happens that the insured person dies before needing long-term care. When shopping for a long-term care policy, consider including different insurance alternatives in your investigation.

For some people long term care insurance is not an option. An elderly person living on a low fixed income may not have enough money to pay the monthly premium for a long term care insurance policy. And long term care insurance is not an option for the person who has been diagnosed with a chronic, debilitating disease.

People in such a position worry that they may need to deplete their life savings, just to pay for a year or two of nursing care.

Both of these problems can be solved by using current law to become qualified for Medicaid. Medicaid is a public assistance program that is funded jointly by the federal and state government. There are state and federal laws governing who may become eligible for the program.

A *Medicaid Qualifying Plan* is a plan that takes both state and federal laws into consideration. Operating within the boundaries of these laws, those who are concerned about becoming impoverished in order to pay for long-term care, seek to preserve and protect their Estate by implementing a Medicaid Qualifying Plan.

There has been controversy about plans designed to qualify a person for Medicaid. Some think that to intentionally arrange finances to qualify for Medicaid is immoral — a legal method of working the system.

Those people may argue: "Why are such things allowed? After all, wasn't Medicaid designed to help poor people? Why should people be allowed to make themselves poor to get on the public dole??

Those who feel they need to qualify for Medicaid have a different point of view. They may argue:

"I worked all my life and hoped to leave a few pennies for the kids. Why did I work so hard? To give it all to a nursing home? I paid my taxes just like everyone else. The government pays hundreds of thousands of dollars for people on Medicare to have open heart surgery, and they pay for lengthy and expensive cancer treatments. Why should those who have Alzheimer's or Parkinson's disease or who suffer a debilitating stroke, not be entitled to receive equal benefits?"

Although we can understand and appreciate both points of view, our job, as we see it, is to just explain the law as it is at the time of publication. We think it is important to do so because many people take a position (pro or con) based on what they perceive the law to be, and not based upon the law as it actually is.

Once the reader understands what it takes to qualify for Medicaid in the state of Georgia, he can decide for himself whether the law is basically fair to the people who need to qualify, or whether it is flawed (either too restrictive or too liberal) and needs to be changed.

Hopefully, those with a strong opinion will share those views with their legislators.

A Medicaid Qualifying Plan 10

A better name for this chapter might be "A Health Care Contingency Plan." A lengthy stay in a nursing home is something most of us do not want to even think about, much less prepare for. Why prepare for something that may never happen? Yet as we age, there is that nagging "What if?" "What if I need long term nursing care? How will I pay for it?"

An effective way to put this anxiety at rest is to have a contingency plan. To form a contingency plan, you need to know your options. In this case, your options are directly related to your ability to pay for that care. But it is hard to predict future fortunes. People win the lottery. Those with a large portfolio may have their fortunes disappear in a market melt-down. There is no need for concern if it turns out that you can afford to pay for your own nursing care; and there is no concern should you become impoverished because there are government programs that provide for your health care. The worst case scenario is that you will be able to afford long-term care, but at the cost of your life savings.

In this chapter we will discuss options available to you under that worst case scenario. We will explain current state and federal law as it relates to qualifying for medical assistance programs.

Once you know the law, you will be able to form a contingency health care plan that is right for you.

WHO IS ENTITLED TO MEDICAID?

Medicaid is a program that provides medical and long term nursing care for people with low income and limited resources. The program is funded and regulated by both federal and state government. The governing agency for the federal government is the Centers for Medicare and Medicaid Services . The **Georgia Department of Community Health** is the state governing agency for the Medicaid program (OCG 49-4-142). Applications are taken and the program administered at the local level by the **Georgia Department of Human Resources, Division of Family and Children Services ("DFCS").**

Medicaid is an entitlement program, meaning that whoever qualifies for the program is entitled to receive benefits under that program. Those who do not qualify are not entitled to any Medicaid benefits.

There are many benefits offered under Medicaid, from health care for mothers and children; to community based services for those who need some assistance with their health care; to full nursing care for those who need assistance with dressing, bathing, eating, walking and toileting. We will limit our discussion of Medicaid to aged persons who are in need of institutional nursing care. You can get information about other Medicaid programs by calling your local DFCS office or (800) 809-7276.

You can also get information about Medicaid from the Georgia Department of Community Health Web site.

 DEPARTMENT OF COMMUNITY HEALTH
http://www.dch.state.ga.us

Persons who are receiving Supplemental Security Income ("SSI") are eligible to receive Medicaid benefits in Georgia because the requirements for these programs are the same. A person who is not receiving SSI, may be eligible for Medicaid if he is 65 or older, or blind, or disabled (Medical Assistance Manual, Volume II ("MA II") Section 2205-1 (MA II/2205-1).

When a person applies for Medicaid (the "Applicant"**) DFCS will investigate his medical condition, income, and assets. If the Applicant is too ill to apply for himself, his spouse, relative, guardian or friend may apply for him (42 US Code of Federal Regulations ("CFR") 435.908, MA II/2050-1).

CITIZENSHIP ELIGIBILITY
To be eligible for Medicaid, the Applicant must be a resident of Georgia, and either a U.S. citizen or an alien who is lawfully admitted for permanent residence (MA II/2215-1).

MEDICAL ELIGIBILITY
Generally an Applicant who has been receiving institutional nursing care for 30 continuous days is medically eligible for Medicaid. In addition to the "length of stay" requirement, there is a "level of care" test as well. DFCS will have the Applicant evaluated to determine whether he requires institutional care. The Applicant can have his own physician make the evaluation. His physician will need to verify, in writing, that the Applicant is in need of institutional care (42 CFR 435.541, MA II/2235-1, 2240-1).

** For simplicity, we will use the male gender for the Applicant and the female gender for his spouse.

As of the year 2005, there is a limit on the amount of income received by the Applicant each month. The Applicant may have no more than $1,737 of countable income each month (MA II/2151-5). If the Applicant is over this *Income Cap* by even one penny, he will be disqualified. However, this problem is easily solved, because the state of Georgia allows the excess income to be placed in a *Qualified Income Trust.* It is also called a *Miller Trust.*

A Qualified Income Trust is a Trust drafted in conformity with state and federal law. Each month the Applicant's excess income is added to the Trust where it is used to help pay for his nursing care. The Trust must be irrevocable with the state of Georgia as the beneficiary of the Trust. If anything remains in the Trust once the Applicant dies, it will be used to reimburse the state for monies spent on his behalf.

An experienced Elder Law attorney will be able to draft the Trust so that it meets DFCS specifications. Once drafted, the Applicant can immediately qualify for Medicaid — provided he meets all other medical and Resource criteria.

The reader may be wondering why the state of Georgia has an Income Cap when it is so easily overcome. The monies placed in the Qualified Income Trust eventually go to the state. Why not (as many other states do) simply require the Applicant to contribute all of his income towards the cost of his nursing care? This is one of those questions to ask your legislator.

THE PERSONAL NEEDS ALLOWANCE

Once the Applicant is approved and becomes a recipient of Medicaid benefits (i.e. a *Medicaid Recipient*), his income is used to supplement the cost of his nursing care. He is allowed to keep a certain amount of his income each month (currently $30) for his personal needs, such as clothing or hair cuts (MA II/A1-3 (2003)).

RESOURCE ELIGIBILITY

Resources are assets owned by the Applicant, either by himself or together with another, that are countable for purposes of qualifying for Medicaid. The Applicant may have no more than $2,000 in Resources. An Applicant who is over the Resource limit needs to "spend down" before he can qualify for Medicaid. His assets are counted as of the first moment of the first day of the month that he enters the long-term care facility and applies for Medicaid. If he is over the Resource limit, he cannot receive Medicaid benefits for that entire month, regardless of whether he reduces his assets during the month so that they are under the limit (MA II/2303-1).

If the Applicant is married, he can transfer anything over $2,000 to his spouse, but there are limits to his spouse's assets as well. If his spouse lives in their home or else-where in the community (i.e., not in a nursing home) she is referred to as the *Community Spouse*.

THE COMMUNITY SPOUSE

The spouse of an Applicant who lives in their home or elsewhere in the community (i.e., not in a nursing home) is called the *Community Spouse*. Prior to 1988, the Community Spouse was required to use whatever assets she had to pay for the nursing care of her spouse. The Applicant could not qualify for Medicaid until they both were virtually impoverished. In addition to being unfair to the Community Spouse, this was not good government policy because it often resulted in the impoverished spouse turning to local government social service programs for support.

The Medicaid provisions of the Medicare Catastrophic Coverage Act of 1988 remedied the situation by considering the assets of the couple as being part of a common pot and allowing the Community Spouse to keep her own share of that pot. The amount allowed has been increased over the years. The federal government allows the Community Spouse to keep up to $95,100 of their combined Resources.

The federal government also considers that the Community Spouse needs money each month for her maintenance. If her income is not sufficient to support her, the income of the Medicaid Recipient will be used to supplement the income of the Community Spouse up to a maximum of $2,377.50 per month. Each year, the federal government adjusts the spouse's Resource allowance and monthly maintenance allowance for cost of living increases. (42 U.S.C. 1382b).

NOTE ⇨ All of the figures used in this Chapter are for the year 2005. The federal and state government adjust these values on a regular basis.

Notice that $95,100 and $2,377.50 are the maximum values set by the federal government in the year 2005. States have the right to administer the Medicaid program according to their state law, provided their state law is within federal guidelines and does not exceed the maximum values set by the federal government. This being the case, the actual amount allowed to the Community spouse can vary significantly state to state.

THE SPOUSE'S INCOME

The state of Georgia uses the federal guideline for the monthly income of the Community Spouse, namely $2,377.50. If her income is less than this amount, she is allowed to keep as much of the Recipient's income each month as is necessary to get her to that maximum value. For example, if the Spouse's only monthly income from Social Security is $1,000, she is allowed to keep up to $1,377.50 each month from the Recipient's monthly income. If for some reason (high medical bills, the need for special care, etc.) she needs more than $2,377.50 a month, she can appeal to have that value increased. The appeal process is explained in the next chapter.

None of the Recipient's income is available to the Community Spouse whose income is greater than $2,377.50. His income will be used to pay for his nursing care. Regardless of the size of the Spouse's income, she is not required to contribute any of her income towards the care of the Applicant (MA II/2554-1).

Property owned by the Applicant, or the Community Spouse, that can be readily converted to cash is considered to be a Resource. This includes bank accounts, certificates of deposit, property in a Revocable Living Trust, stocks, bonds, and so on (MA II/2300-2). The state of Georgia uses the federal guideline $95,100, meaning that the Community Spouse is allowed to keep up to $95,100 as the **Community Spouse Resource Allowance** (42 U.S.C. 1396r-5(c)(2), 1396r-5f).

But suppose the Applicant and his spouse have $200,000 worth of assets between them. In that case, the Community Spouse can keep $95,100 as her Resource Allowance. The Applicant can keep his $2,000, but that leaves them with $102,900 above the Resource limit.

$$\$200,000 - \$95,100 - \$2,000 = \$102,900$$

The first question to ask in such a situation is whether all of their assets count as a Resource.

Some items owned by the Applicant, or his spouse, can be converted to cash, but are not counted as a Resource. Such items are considered to be "Exempt Assets" or "Non-Countable Resources." We will refer to them as **Excluded Resources** (42 U.S.C. 1382b).

EXCLUDED RESOURCES

In the state of Georgia, the following items are Excluded Resources and are not counted as a Resource for purposes of determining Medicaid Eligibility for the Applicant.

HOUSEHOLD GOODS AND PERSONAL EFFECTS

Household items and personal effects being used by the Applicant or his Community Spouse are Excluded Resources. They include:

⇨ wedding and engagement rings, regardless of their value;

⇨ home furnishings and appliances, books, and household tools

Coin, stamp or art collections that are worth significant amount of money, may be counted by DFCS as a Resource (MA II/2319-1, II/2399-6, II/2399-7).

MOTOR VEHICLES

All cars owned by the Applicant or his Community Spouse are Excluded Resources (MA II/2308).

LIFE INSURANCE

⇨ An insurance policy owned by the Applicant is an Excluded Resource, provided its face value (the amount paid at death) is $5,000 or less (MA II/2399-9, II/2323-1).

If the face value of the policy greater is than $5,000, the cash surrender value of the policy is counted as a Resource. You can write to the insurance company and they will give you the current cash surrender value.

A Term Life Insurance policy has no cash surrender value, so such policy is not counted as a Resource regardless of its face value.

THE HOME

⇨ The primary residence (home, condominium, co-operative apartment, or mobile home) that is occupied by the Applicant or his family (spouse, minor or dependent child, dependent relative) is an Excluded Resource.

The Applicant's home is an Excluded Resource so long as it is his primary residence or that of his spouse or dependent family member. If the Applicant is in a nursing home, and no family member lives in the home, it continues to be an Excluded Resource, provided the Applicant, or someone acting on his behalf, has indicated, in writing, that the Applicant intends to return home (MA II/2316-1).

INCOME PRODUCING PROPERTY

⇨ Business property that is essential for the support of the Applicant and/or his Community Spouse is an Excluded Resource (MA II/2327-1).

⇨ Real property owned by the Applicant or his Community Spouse that is not occupied as their home does not count as a Resource, provided it is producing income that is essential for the support of the Applicant or his spouse. For example, a summer cottage used for summer vacations, counts as a Resource; but a cottage that is rented out and the income is used for their support, does not count as a Resource (MA II/2399-11).

⇨ The cash value of any tax qualified retirement plan, such as a 401K plan, does not count as a Resource, provided the Applicant is receiving periodic payments. A retirement plan that belongs to the Community Spouse is an Excluded Resource, regardless of whether payments are currently being made (MA II/2332-1, 2399-11).

BURIAL ARRANGEMENTS

⇨ Burial spaces for the Applicant or his family (spouse child, parent, sibling and the spouse of a family member) are Excluded Resources. This includes prepaid burial space items such as grave sites, mausoleums, urns, niches, etc. Opening and closing the grave, headstones, and headstone engravings are also considered burial space items.

⇨ A Preneed Funeral Contract as described in Chapter 8 is an Excluded Resource. Because the contract is revocable, the funds are accessible to the Applicant. DFCS will carefully review the Preneed Contract to determine whether the amount paid is reasonable or whether the Applicant is attempting to improperly shelter excess Resources.

⇨ A burial fund of up to $5,000 for the Applicant and a burial fund of $5,000 for the Community Spouse are Excluded Resources provided the funds are kept is in a separate bank account and clearly identified as a burial account (MA II/2312-1, II/2399-2).

ASSETS THAT ARE NOT SALEABLE

⇨   Property owned by the Applicant or his spouse must be able to be converted to cash in order to be counted as a Resource. Shares held in a *close corporation*, (i.e. a small private corporation whose shares have no market value), Life Estate interests, certain irrevocable annuities, and other non-saleable items can be considered as an Excluded Resource, subject to the approval of DFCS (MA II/2300-1).

JOINTLY OWNED ASSETS

The DFCS considers the full value of a bank account owed jointly by the Applicant (or his spouse) to be available to the Applicant, unless it can be proven that the other joint owner contributed to the account. For example, if the Applicant owns a joint account with his son, the entire balance counts as a Resource unless the son can prove that he contributed his own money to that account. The son's net contribution (how much he contributed less how much he withdrew) does not count as a Resource, however, DFCS may require that the son withdraw that amount from the account (MA II/2334-4).

OTHER EXCLUDED RESOURCES

We listed many of the more common items that DFCS considers to be Excluded Resources. But this is not a complete list. There are other items that DFCS will not count as part of the Applicant's Resources. An experienced Elder Law Attorney will be able to examine all of the property owned by Applicant or his spouse and explain which of these assets DFCS considers to be an Excluded Resource.

THE SPEND-DOWN OPTION

Now that we know what does (and does not) count as a Resource, the next question is what options are available to our couple who are over the Resource limit by $102,9000. Those with no knowledge of the law, might think the only option available to this couple is to pay for his nursing care until the $102,900 runs out. Those who carefully read the previous pages, might suggest that the couple check to see whether they can use the money to purchase items that do not count as a Resource.

Both state and federal law allow the Applicant and his Community Spouse to use their excess Resources to purchase Excludable Resources, without losing the right to receive Medicaid benefits, provided they pay a fair market value for the item. This being the case, the couple can make funeral or burial arrangements, if they have not already done so. They can purchase household items such as furniture, a television set, a new refrigerator or stove, etc.

REPAIRING EXEMPT ITEMS

Paying money to repair an Exempt Resource is a good spend-down strategy. Perhaps the Exempt family car needs new brakes, or tires. The Community Spouse may decide to replace the Exempt car with a new model.

If the house is in need of repair or improvement, this is the time to fix it up. A new heating, plumbing, electric or security system can use up funds quickly.

SPEND-DOWN BY TRANSFER TO DISABLED PERSON

As explained in Chapter 7, if a child is receiving Social Security disability benefits, the parent can transfer money to a Community Trust for the child. This transfer will not disqualify the child, or the parent, from receiving government benefits, provided the Trust is drafted according to state and federal law (MA II/2342-3).

SPEND-DOWN BY PAYING DEBTS

Some sceptics might think $102,900 is a lot of money to spend down. Maybe the couple previously made all funeral arrangements. Perhaps they really don't need (or want) new furniture or appliances. In such case, the solution may be to pay off all of their outstanding debts. Paying off loans is a valid spend-down strategy because it is just a return of monies given to the Applicant by the lender for the purchase of an Excluded Resource (car, house, clothing, household items).

The Applicant, or his Community Spouse, will need to prove to DFCS that the monies spent were used to pay off a valid debt. If he paid a credit card debt, DFCS will want to see the contract with the company and the monthly statement showing what items were purchased. If the money was used to pay down a mortgage on his home, DFCS will want to see the original loan documents as well as a statement showing the new balance, or a satisfaction of mortgage, if it was paid in full.

MAYBE SPEND-DOWN IS NOT NECESSARY

Suppose the couple with too much in Resources has too little income. For example, suppose it is determined that the Community Spouse needs at least $2,377.50 per month, but the couple's combined income is only $1,500. In such case, she can ask DFCS to allow her to keep as much of couple's excess assets as is necessary to give her this minimum income. In effect, she needs to ask "May I keep more than my Resource Allowance so that the income from this property will help to get me to that minimum income?"

It is the legal right of the Community Spouse to receive the minimum Needs Allowance allowed by both state and federal government. It is reasonable to ask DFCS to allow her keep as much of their Resources as necessary to achieve that income, even if it means keeping more than allowed as a Resource Allowance. But it will take the assistance of an experienced Elder Law attorney to convince DFCS that allowing her to keep more in Resources is a proper thing to do.

If DFCS denies the request, it will be necessary to go through an Appeals process to decide the issue. The Appeals process can drag on for months. Meanwhile, the status of the Applicant remains in limbo. Because of the legal cost of the Appeal and the uncertainty of whether the Court will agree that this is a genuine case of undue hardship and that additional Resources are necessary for the support of the Community Spouse, it may be better to use a spend-down strategy that enables the Spouse to obtain additional income. One such strategy is the MEDICAID ANNUITY. The Community Spouse uses the excess Resources to buy an Annuity that will give her additional income. This spend-down strategy is permissible, provided it conforms to Georgia and federal law.

A spend-down strategy that is currently allowed by both federal and state law is the purchase of an *Immediate Pay Annuity*; i.e., an Annuity whose payments begin the month after the purchase and continues for a fixed period of time. For purposes of Medicaid eligibility, that fixed period of time must be less than, or equal to, the life expectancy of the Annuitant (in this case, the Community Spouse). She can name a Successor Annuitant to receive the payments in the event she dies earlier than her life expectancy.

The life expectancy of the Annuitant is determined by
Life Expectancy Tables—Males and
Life Expectancy Tables—Females
as published in the Medical Assistance Manual (MA II/ 2339-3).

You can find excerpts from that table at the Public Service Information section of the Eagle Publishing Company Web site.   http://www.eaglepublishing.com

By purchasing an Immediate Pay Annuity, the excess Resources are converted to a monthly income that continues for the term of the policy.

In order to qualify as a permissible spend-down strategy, the annuity must meet both state and federal criteria; specifically:

UNASSIGNABLE AND IRREVOCABLE
The Annuity contract cannot be transferred, sold or assigned. It must be irrevocable. In other words, nothing can be changed; not the monthly payment, nor the number of payments, nor the identity of the Annuitant (MA II/2339-1).

NO CASH VALUE

The Annuity contract must have no value other than the monthly payments to the annuitant.

ACTUARIALLY SOUND

The Annuity contract must be *actuarially sound,* meaning that the money invested in the Annuity must be returned to the Annuitant in equal monthly payments. The duration of the payments must be equal to or less than his life expectancy. The life expectancy figures must be as printed in the Medical Assistance Manual.

There is no rounding "up." For example, according to the Life Expectancy Tables, a 65 year old man has a life expectancy of 14.96 years. An Annuity that makes regular payments to the Annuitant for 14 years is considered to be actuarially sound, but an Annuity that makes payments for 15 years is not.

We will refer to an Annuity that meets all of these criteria (no cash value, unassignable, irrevocable, actuarially sound) as a *Medicaid Annuity*.

 VERIFY THAT THE ANNUITY MEETS DFCS CRITERIA PRIOR TO PURCHASE

Once the Annuity is purchased it is irrevocable, so before you buy it, have an Elder Law attorney, or the agent who is selling the Annuity, check with DFCS to be sure the Annuity meets state and federal requirements. If you purchase the Annuity and for some reason DFCS determines it does not meet current state and federal criteria, the amount paid for the Annuity might count as an impermissible transfer of assets and a **PENALTY PERIOD** of ineligibility will be imposed, i.e., a period of time that the Applicant is disqualified from receiving Medicaid benefits. The Penalty Period is discussed later in this chapter.

Purchasing a Medicaid Annuity could solve the problem for the Community Spouse who has too little income and too much in Resources. She can use her excess Resources to buy the Annuity. She will keep the income from that investment, just as she would if she had invested in a stock, bond or Certificate of Deposit. Unlike such investments, part of the money she paid for the Annuity is returned to her each month along with interest. Most importantly, the Annuity does not count as a Resource.

This spend-down strategy can be used by the Community Spouse even when her income is not a problem. But it may not make economic sense if the sum of her monthly income, including the income from the annuity, exceeds $2,377.50. For example, suppose she has a monthly income of $2,000. The DFCS will allow her to keep up to 377.50 of her husband's income. If the annuity pays $377.50 (or more), she may keep none of her husband's income. All of his income will be used for his nursing care. In other words, purchasing the Medicaid Annuity may enable the Applicant to qualify for Medicaid, but it may not result in extra income for the Community Spouse.

And there are other things to consider.
⇨ RISK OF LOSS
By purchasing an Annuity, the Community Spouse is giving her money to a company in exchange for the company's promise to return part of the principal each month, together with interest. The company promises to make these payments every month for a certain number of years. Should the company become bankrupt during that period of time, the monies invested might be lost.

⇨ LOSS OF LIQUIDITY
Should the Applicant die shortly after she buys the Annuity, his Community Spouse cannot cash it in. She must keep the investment for the full term.

⇨ FIXED RETURN ON INVESTMENT

Annuities offer a fixed rate of return on the money invested and there is no way to adjust that rate for periods of inflation. The rate of return on the Annuity is set at the time of purchase. We are currently in a period of low interest rates, but there are inflationary pressures at work that can operate to quickly increase interest rates. Should of interest rates go into the double digit range, the Annuity will still yield the same single digit rate of return as when it was purchased.

⇨ THE COMMUNITY SPOUSE MAY NEED NURSING CARE

Buying a Medicaid Annuity for a Community Spouse who is herself aged or in frail health may not be the best option. It could happen that she needs long-term nursing care and will need to apply for Medicaid. If she purchases an Annuity and later becomes a Medicaid Recipient, that extra income will be used as her contribution to her nursing care.

Needless to say, all these concerns need to be addressed before investing in a Medicaid Annuity. Consultation with an Elder Law attorney prior to the purchase is a must.

NOT THE BEST OPTION FOR THE SINGLE APPLICANT

Although purchasing a Medicaid Annuity may work for a healthy Community Spouse with a low fixed income, it may not be the best strategy for the single Applicant, because any income he receives from the Annuity will be used for his nursing care. He could live in the nursing home longer than his life expectancy and all the money invested in the Annuity would be used for his care.

One exception may be the single Applicant who intends to return home after a few months. For example, suppose an unmarried father with $100,000 needs extensive nursing care because of a car accident. If doctors expect he will be able to return home after several months of therapy and nursing care, he might consider purchasing a Medicaid Annuity for $98,000. He can name his child to be the beneficiary of the Annuity should he die before he receives his final Annuity payment.

Once he makes the purchase, he can immediately apply for Medicaid. He will of course report the purchase to DFCS. The DFCS will examine the terms of the Annuity to be sure they satisfy current regulations. If they do and he meets all other requirements, he should qualify for Medicaid.

He's happy because he did not need to spend down his $98,000 in nursing home bills. He's hoping that his condition improves enough so that he can return home. In such case, his nursing care will be paid by Medicaid, and he will continue to receive the income from the Annuity when he returns home. The DFCS is happy because any income he receives while in the facility will go toward payment of his nursing home bill; leaving that much less for DFCS to contribute to his care.

His child may, or may not, think this is the best solution depending upon whether he thinks his father will need nursing care longer than expected. By purchasing a Medicaid Annuity, his father is betting that he will not need nursing care for the rest of his life expectancy. If he loses his bet, none of his assets are protected. All of his money will be used to pay for his nursing care. In such case it may be better for him to use a strategy better designed for the single Applicant.

Spend-down may not be the best strategy for the single Applicant with significant assets such as the father who has $100,000. Sure he can make his funeral arrangements; but that will only use up a small portion of his assets. He could buy an expensive car, but what good would that be if he needs to enter a nursing home? The Medicaid Annuity is a possibility, but if he has a progressive, long-term disease such as Alzheimer's or Parkinson, and needs to go into a facility, he could very well live longer than his life expectancy and all the money invested in the Annuity would be used for his care.

If the Applicant has a medical condition that does not require immediate nursing care, he may decide to simply transfer all of his money to his child. The DFCS will consider this to be an ***uncompensated transfer*** i.e. the Applicant gets nothing in return for the transfer (love and affection don't count).

Should the Applicant go this route, DFCS will disqualify the Applicant from receiving Medicaid for a period of time based on the amount that was transferred. The period of time that the Applicant is disqualified is called the ***Penalty Period*** or the ***Period of Ineligibility***.

The rule for computing the Penalty Period is fairly complex, but in general, the Penalty Period is computed by dividing the amount transferred by the average monthly cost of nursing home care in the state of Georgia. The value for the average monthly cost of nursing care used by DFCS in the year 2005 is $4,167.33.

If the Applicant in the example just given, decided to transfer all of his $100,000 to his child he would be disqualified for months
$$\$100,000 / \$4,167.33 = 23.99 \text{ months}$$
The DFCS rounds this down to the nearest month.

But 23 months is a long time. It could happen that the father needs nursing care before the Penalty Period is up. In that case the child will need return the money so that the father can pay for his stay in the nursing home.

The DFCS allows the Penalty Period to be reduced provided the money is returned to the Applicant (MA II/2342-2). For example, suppose our Applicant transferred the $100,0000 and six months later he needs nursing care. The Penalty Period for $25,003.97 of the transferred funds has expired $4,167.33 x 6 = $25,003.97

If the difference ($74,996.03) is returned to the father, there will be no further penalty. However, this is not a complete solution because the father still has too much to qualify for Medical Assistance Programs. He will need to spend down his assets (probably on nursing home care) before he can qualify for Medicaid. In such case, the Applicant cannot preserve all of his assets, but he should be able to preserve much of what he owns by making successive gifts to his child.

THE MONTHLY PENALTY RULE

The strategy for the *Monthly Penalty Rule* is simple. The Applicant enters the nursing home as a private paying patient. Each month he pays for the cost of his care. Each month he makes a gift to his child. The gift must not incur a Penalty Period greater than a single month. Currently, a gift of $8,334.66 will trigger a two month Penalty Period, so the gift in any given month must be less than that value. For example, if the father gives away $8,000, there is only a one month penalty:

$$\$8,000/\$4,167.33 = 1.92 \text{ or } 1 \text{ month}$$

Each month his Resources are reduced by the gift made to his son and the cost of his nursing care. Each month he is disqualified from applying for that month. If he uses $3,000 of his savings each month to pay for the cost of his nursing care and he makes a gift of $8,000 each month to his child, he will reduce his Resources each month by $11,000. An Applicant who has $100,000 should be eligible to apply for Medicaid in 9 months ($11,000 X 9 = $99,000) with $72,000 going to his son ($8,000 X 9 = $72,000).

 DO IT RIGHT OR SUFFER THE FULL PENALTY

The time of the transfer is critical. The sum total of the gifts made in any given month must not exceed the one month Penalty Period. If the gift periods overlap, or two gifts are made in the same month that add up to more than a one month penalty, the gifts will count as a single transferer with full penalty for that transfer.

Best to have an Elder Law attorney supervise the gifting schedule. He will compute the maximum value that you can gift under current values being used for private pay nursing care.

JUST GIVE IT ALL AWAY

The strategy we have been discussing can be used if the Applicant needs nursing care in the near future. But it may happen that a person is diagnosed in the early stages of a progressive disease that is expected to ultimately result in a lengthy stay in a nursing facility. A person in such a situation may decide to give his property away, with the hope that he will not need long term nursing care for at least three years.

Three years is the **Look Back Period** that DFCS uses to investigate the finances of a person who applies for Medicaid. The Look Back Period starts on the date the Applicant enters the nursing facility and applies for Medicaid and goes back three years from that date. The Look Back Period increases to five years, if there was a transfer into a Trust (42 U.S.C. 1396p(c); MA II/2342-1). If DFCS determines that the Applicant, or his Community Spouse, made an uncompensated transfer during the Look Back Period, they will impose a Penalty Period.

 THERE IS NO LIMIT ON THE PENALTY PERIOD

Although DFCS will only look back three years for transfers, there is no limit on the Penalty Period imposed for that transfer. For example, suppose the Applicant gives his child $300,000. If he applies for Medicaid within three years from the date of transfer, he can be denied Medicaid benefits for almost six years:

$$\$300,000 / \$4,167.33 = 71.99 \text{ months}$$
$$71/12 = 5.92 \text{ years}$$

Of course the way to avoid the problem is to transfer the funds and not apply within the Look Back Period. But if the transfer was made into an irrevocable Trust during the Look Back Period, the Applicant may be stuck with the full 71 months; because, as discussed, if funds were transferred into a Trust, the state has the right to look back five years and impose the full penalty for the transfer.

And this is not a game of "Catch me if you can." Under both state and federal law, the Applicant and his spouse (or whoever applies for him) are required to make a full disclosure of transfers made during these periods. Anyone who knowingly and wilfully makes a false statement in an application for Medicaid can be convicted for Medicaid fraud. All benefits must be repaid. If the amount is over $500, the person can be convicted of a felony and imprisoned for up to five years (OCG 49-4-15).

The reader may be thinking "Yes, but if I don't make a transfer into a Trust, all the law requires is that I report transfers made within the previous three years. If I come down with an illness that I know will cause me to deteriorate over a period of time, all I need do is give all my money to my child; be sure to wait three years and I will qualify for Medicaid. My child will keep my money safe. Should I need that money, my child will return as much as I need. Money that I don't use will be protected for my child."

The Medicaid Qualifying Plan of giving away all assets and then waiting three years is certainly allowed under the law, but this is a "brute force" approach to the problem. There's no finesse. It is a drastic step to take and fraught with peril. Once the money is transferred, a completed gift is made.

The child becomes the legal owner of the money and with all of the obvious "what ifs."

What if the child goes bankrupt or dies?

What if the child is sued? Will a Court order the child to use the money you gave to pay the judgment?

What if the child is divorced? Will the Court decide that your child's spouse is entitled to half of that money?

But the real problem is the loss of independence. Being impoverished at a time in your life when you are unable to supplement your income, and when your physical health is declining, can lead to much sadness. Imagine going to your child and asking for money. Imagine the child thinking, or worse yet, asking
"What's the money for?"

And what if you give the money away and never need nursing care? Medical technology is advancing with amazing speed. Although few cures have been found for mankind's ills, there have been many breakthroughs in their treatment. With modern drugs, many patients are now able to function without the need for long-term care. Even those who have been diagnosed with a progressive disease may not need nursing care for several years — maybe never.

Meanwhile, the money is gone, and your independence along with it.

Giving away all one's money and then waiting three years may work, but at the cost of your independence. Putting money into an irrevocable Trust and waiting five years has its risks. A lot can happen in that time. You could require full nursing care the day after you transfer your assets into the Trust. Maybe the five year look-back is changed to a six year look back period.

For those in good health, an alternative is to do nothing until you actually need nursing home care and then implement a Medicaid qualifying strategy at that time. Of course, there is the chance that you take suddenly ill, say with a stroke, and are unable to implement a Medicaid Qualifying plan. A Durable Power Of Attorney that is properly drafted and signed while you have capacity should solve the problem. You can appoint someone to be your Attorney In Fact to implement a Medicaid Qualifying plan for you.

It is important that the Durable Power of Attorney be properly drafted. In December 2002, A New Jersey Court refused to allow a son to transfer property on behalf of his incapacitated mother for the purpose of qualifying for Medicaid. Although his mother gave him a Power of Attorney authorizing him to apply for Medicaid on her behalf, the Court refused to allow the transfer because the Power of Attorney "... did not provide for him to make gifts on her behalf to himself or anyone else, either to qualify her for Medicaid or for any other reason" (*In the Matter of Mildred Keri*, Superior Court of New Jersey, Appellate Division, A-5949-01T5). This case was reversed by the New Jersey Supreme Court and eventually the son was able to transfer the assets on behalf of his mother. But a transfer of property under an improperly drafted Power of Attorney can still be challenged.

DFCS may challenge transfers made under a Power of Attorney that does not give the Attorney In Fact specific authority to implement a Medicaid Qualifying plan. It is important that your Power of Attorney be drafted by an Elder Law attorney who knows what provisions to include in the document so that it will stand up to DFCS scrutiny.

 THE ONLY THING CERTAIN IS CHANGE

The discussion relating to Medicaid Qualifying Plans for the state of Georgia is not intended to lull the reader into a false sense of security. The only thing certain about federal and state laws is that they will change. Whatever strategy you choose may not be around when you need it. For example, there are those who oppose the use of the Medicaid Annuity. Legislation has been proposed in several states that would restrict its use. Some states, such as Alabama, Idaho and Kansas currently have laws that limit the use of the Annuity as a Medicaid qualifying option.

More importantly, there is a proposal in the federal government to give states new powers to reduce, eliminate or increase Medicaid benefits within the state. Under this proposal, benefits for welfare recipients, poor children and other groups who are automatically eligible for Medicaid would remain regulated by federal law. The state would be given autonomy to administer the Medicaid program for other groups; and in particular for the elderly in need of nursing care. Proponents of state autonomy explain that with autonomy, the state could increase benefits, but in these days of budget deficits, more likely the states will opt to decrease Medicaid benefits to the elderly.

If states are given autonomy in administering the long-term nursing care program, uniformity would no longer be imposed by the federal government. Medicaid benefits for the elderly could vary significantly state to state. Not only would there be variation state to state, there could be variation within the state. State programs could be administered with different eligibility criteria county to county. There could even be a difference in benefits county to county.

The point is that there is no certainty when it comes to future Medicaid qualifying options.

But we did not write this chapter to give the reader a definitive Medicaid Qualifying strategy. Rather, it was to give the reader an understanding of the law as it relates to qualifying for Medicaid; and to let the reader know that under current law, options are available should the need for long-term nursing care arise in the future.

We also wrote this chapter to let the general public understand how this federal program is administered here in the state of Georgia. And, incidentally, we touched only on the basics. There are other, more sophisticated, Medicaid Qualifying options available that an experienced Elder Law attorney can explain to you. The prudent thing to do is to visit an Elder Law attorney if and when you become concerned about a long term care problem. He can explain current law to you as it relates to qualifying for Medicaid. He can suggest the best path for you to follow, given your set of circumstances.

It is also important to keep up with changes in policy both in the state and federal government; and to let your legislators know how you feel about such changes.

Protecting the Homestead 11

As explained in Chapter 10, whether a home in the name of the Applicant counts as Resource for purposes of qualifying for Medicaid depends on his spouse or a dependent family member is living there. Even if no family member occupies the home, the Applicant cannot be denied Medicaid benefits because he owns a home, provided he says he intends to return to his home. However, once he qualifies for Medicaid and receives benefits, the state has the right to have a physician determine whether he can reasonably be expected to return home. If not, the state has a right to place a TEFRA LIEN on the property for monies spent on his behalf. TEFRA stands for TAX EQUITY AND FISCAL RESPONSIBILITY ACT, a federal law. Once the lien is recorded, the property cannot be sold or transferred until money spent by the state for the care of the homeowner is treturned to the state.

Even if the state does not place a lien on his home during his lifetime, if the Medicaid Recipient received Medical Assistance after age 55, the state can place a Tefra Lien on the property and seek recovery from the sale of his home once he dies. The state will not place a lien on the property or seek recovery from a home owned by a deceased Recipient while his spouse, or minor or disabled child are living there. However, once the child reaches 21, or the spouse and disabled child are deceased, whoever inherits the home will need to pay off the lien or the state can force the sale of the property and take the money from the proceeds of the sale (42 U.S.C. 1396p, OCG 49-4-147.1).

In this chapter we discuss ways to protect the home from a TEFRA Lien.

TRANSFERRING THE HOME

Protecting the homestead is easy to do if the Medicaid Recipient is married. Under state and federal law, the Applicant can transfer his home to the Community Spouse without penalty. He can make the transfer either before or after he applies for Medicaid (42 U.S.C. 1396p (c) 2A), MA II/2342-3).

If the home is in the name of the Medicaid Recipient only, he can sign a deed transferring the property to his spouse. If he and the Community Spouse own the property jointly, they can sign a deed transferring the property to the Community Spouse. It is important to make the transfer of the joint interest because the state can place seek recovery from the Recipient's "half" once he dies. In the event the Community Spouse dies first, the state has the right to place a TEFRA Lien on the entire value of the home.

Protecting the home is more of a problem for the aged, single parent; and it is a problem for aging parents who both are not in the best of health. Who knows which of them will require long term nursing care? Maybe both will need such care. Maybe neither of them will require nursing care. Most parents want to have their children inherit the one thing the parent has of value, namely their home. Parents fear that if they ever need Medicaid benefits, their home will be sold to reimburse the state. This idea is so distressing to some parents that even though they are in relatively good health, they may decide to transfer their home to their child with the understanding that the parents will continue to live there for the rest of their lives. Those planning such a move need to understand that they are trading one risk (need to apply for Medicaid) for several other risks.

⊠ RISK OF LOSS

Once you transfer the property to your child it becomes his property and that property can be lost or used to pay for his debts just like anything else he owns. Your child could run into serious financial difficulties. Your child could be sued. This is especially a risk if your child is a professional (doctor, nurse, accountant, financial planner, attorney, etc.). If your child is found to be personally liable for damages, your home could become part of the settlement of that law suit.

If your child is (or gets) married, this complicates matters even more. If the child divorces, the value of your home might be included as part of the property settlement agreement. This may be to your child's detriment because the child may need to share the value of the property with his/her former spouse. If you do not transfer the property, it cannot become part of the marital equation.

Even if your child is single there is a risk of loss. Your child may want to take out a business loan. If the loan is significant, the lender will want to include everything your child owns as collateral (security for the debt). If the lender learns that you are occupying the house, he will especially want to include your house as collateral because that will motivate your son to repay the loan.

The point is, transferring the house to your child could be bad for both of you. And that is not the only downside.

⊠ LOSS OF HOMESTEAD TAX EXEMPTION

In Georgia, those who own and occupy real property as their residence are entitled to a *Homestead Tax Exemption*. Additional exemptions are available for the disabled veteran, or for those who are over 62 with low income (OCG 48-4-44, 48-5-47). If you transfer your homestead, you will lose your right to receive these tax breaks.

⊠ LOSS OF HOMESTEAD CREDITOR PROTECTION

Up to $5,000 of the value of your homestead is protected from creditors during your lifetime. This may not seem much, but it could keep a roof over your head if the equity in your home is under $5,000. For example, suppose your home is worth $70,000 and you have a mortgage of $65,000. Except for mechanics liens and taxes, no one can force the sale of your home (OCG 44-13-1). If you simply transfer your homestead to a child, you lose your homestead protection against creditors. If you are married, it is a double loss of creditor protection. Not only do you lose creditor protection for yourself, you lose it for your spouse as well (see Chapter 5).

If the child does not occupy that property as his home, there is no homestead creditor protection what-soever. The child's creditors can force the sale of the property (that's your home) for a relatively small amount of unpaid debt.

⊠ POSSIBLE GIFT TAX

A federal Gift Tax needs to be paid if the value of the equity in your home (plus the value of all the gifts you gave over your lifetime in excess of the Annual Gift Tax Exclusion) exceeds the lifetime Gift Tax Exclusion. The current lifetime federal Gift Tax Exclusion is $1,000,000, so for most of us, this is not a problem. Yet there still is the hassle of filing a Gift Tax return.

⊠ POSSIBLE CAPITAL GAINS TAX

Although Congress has expressed its intent to phase out the Estate Tax, there is no discussion to do away with the Capital Gains Tax. If you gift the property to the child during your lifetime, when he sells the property he will pay a Capital Gains Tax on the increase in value from the price you paid for your home to the selling price at the time your child sells the property.

If you do not make the gift during your lifetime, the child will inherit the property with a step-up in basis, i.e., he will inherit the property at its market value as of the date of your death. Under today's tax structure and continuing until 2009, that step-up in basis is unlimited. If your child sells the property when he inherits it, he will pay no Capital Gains Tax, regardless of how large the step-up in basis.

In 2010, there will be a limit on the amount that can be inherited free of the Capital Gains Tax, but that limit is quite high so for most of us this is not a concern.

⊠ POSSIBLE LOSS OF GOVERNMENT BENEFITS

If you are married and you transfer property to someone other than your spouse, then depending upon the value of the transfer, both you and your spouse could be disqualified from receiving Medicaid or Supplemental Security Income ("SSI") if you apply within three years from the date of transfer of the property. That increases to five years if you transfer the property into a Trust. It could happen that during that period of time, one of you takes suddenly ill and requires long-term nursing care.

Why jeopardize your right to receive Medicaid for both of you? Owning a homestead will not disqualify you from receiving Medicaid, but transferring it may make you and your spouse ineligible for a long time.

The elderly parent, who is single, may not be convinced that gifting the house is a bad idea. He may be thinking "By giving my home to my child, I risk not being able to qualify for Medicaid for three years. If I don't make the gift and need Medicaid at any time during the rest of my lifetime, the state will get the house for sure."

But there are better Estate Plans than the outright gift. The Life Estate strategy may be one of them.

You can give the property to your child, and keep a Life Estate for yourself. Your child will have no right to your homestead while you are alive so you have no fear that the property can be lost or taken from you during your lifetime. Upon your death, your child will own the property 100%, and without the need for Probate.

Depending on the value of your home, this Life Estate approach might allow you to shorten the Medicaid transfer Penalty Period, because you are not giving your child the full value of your home, you are just giving away the value of the **Remainder Interest** i.e., what is left of the property after your death.

The value of the Remainder Interest depends on your life expectancy. A gift of a Remainder Interest when you are 90 is worth more to your child than when you are 50. The only question that remains is how the DFCS will evaluate the transfer of the property to your child.

DETERMINING THE VALUE OF THE REMAINDER INTEREST

The DFCS publishes values for the Life Estate Interest and the Remainder Interest based on the age of the Grantor at the time of the transfer UNISEX LIFE ESTATE OR REMAINDER INTEREST TABLE (MA II/2322-3).

You can find excerpts from this table, at the Information section of the Eagle Publishing Company Web site.
http://www.eaglepublishing.com

Fortunately, this table goes up to age 109, so the value they assign to the remainder interest is relatively low. For example, according to this table, if a 70 year old makes a transfer to his son and keeps a Life Estate for himself, his Life Estate is equal to 61% of the value of the property. The remainder interest is worth only 39%.

The actual percentage given in the table for the Remainder Interest is .39478. If the father's *equity in the home* (fair market value less monies owed) is $100,000, it means the value of the gift of the Remainder Interest is $39,478.

This greatly reduces the Penalty Period. If he transferred the house and did not keep a Life Estate, his Penalty Period would be 23 months:

$$\$100,000/\$4,167.33 = 23 \text{ months}$$

By keeping a Life Estate that Penalty Period reduces to 9 months: $39,478/$4,167.33 = 9.47 or 9 months.

 ### THE LIFE ESTATE IS NOT A COMPLETE SOLUTION

A Life Estate is a better Medicaid Qualifying Plan than an outright gift but only for purposes of shortening the period of ineligibility. Issues of control and taxes and recovery still remain.

CONTROL
You will not be able to sell your home, or get a mortgage on the property, without permission from your child.

TAX ISSUES
And, as explained at the end of Chapter 2, if you sell the home, you might need to pay a Capital Gains Tax.

RECOVERY BY THE STATE

Under Federal law, the state has the right to recover monies spent on your behalf if you received nursing care under Medicaid after the age of 55. Monies can be recovered from property you own at the time of your death. This includes property you own jointly with another, and property in which you own a Life Estate interest. It does not include property in which your brother or sister own an interest in your home, provided your sibling lived in the home at least one year before you entered a nursing home and qualified for Medicaid (42 U.S.C. 1396p(b)(4)(B), Rule 111-3-8-.07 of Department of Community Health Medical Assistance ("DCHMA")).

Up until the year 2004, the state of Georgia did not actively seek recovery. But as of August 5, 2004, the RULES OF DEPARTMENT OF COMMUNITY HEALTH MEDICAL ASSISTANCE, Chapter 111-3-8 Estate Recovery, went into effect. Those rules mandate that the state of Georgia seek recovery according to state and federal law.

Estates valued at $25,000 or less are exempt form Estate Recovery because it is not cost effective for the state of Georgia to pursue recovery (Rules 111-3-8.02(4) DCHMA).

TRANSFERS THAT PROTECT

As explained, you can own a home and still qualify for Medicaid, but there still is the concern that once you become a Medicaid recipient, the state may place a TEFRA Lien on your homestead for monies spent on your behalf. Under current law, there are several ways to protect your home from such lien. For a married person, the home can be protected by transferring it to the Community Spouse.

TRANSFERRING THE HOME TO THE SPOUSE

The Applicant is free to transfer his home to his spouse either before or after he qualifies for Medicaid. Once the house is in the name of the Community Spouse, she can arrange to have it inherited by a family member and not the Medicaid Recipient. Should the Applicant be too ill to make the transfer himself, then the deed can be signed by his Attorney-In-Fact under a properly drafted Durable Power of Attorney. If he did not give an Attorney-In-Fact authority to make the transfer, and he is too ill to sign his name, it may be necessary to have a Conservator who can ask the Court for permission to make the transfer.

Establishing a conservatorship be expensive and time consuming, but it is important that the homestead be transferred to the Community Spouse because it could happen that the Community Spouse dies first leaving the home in the name of the now single Medicaid recipient. The downside is that there is no guarantee that the judge will allow the transfer of the homestead to the Community Spouse. Before you apply for a conservatorship it is important to ask your attorney whether such transfers have been allowed in the past.

TRANSFERRING THE HOME TO A SIBLING

Under state and federal law, if an Applicant owns his home together with a sibling and the sibling lived with the Applicant for at least one year before entering the nursing facility, the Applicant can transfer the home to the sibling without a Medicaid transfer penalty (42 U.S.C. 1396p, MA II/2342-3). This law presents an opportunity for an unmarried Applicant who has a brother or sister to protect the homestead. The only question is how the sibling becomes co-owner. If the Applicant and his sibling purchased the property together, and the sibling lived in the home for a year prior to the Applicant entering the nursing home, then the sibling's interest in the property is protected. The Applicant can transfer his share of the homestead to his sibling without penalty, and that will protect all of the homestead.

If the house is in the Applicant's name only, then it is important to consult with an Elder Law attorney to determine the best way for the sibling to become part owner of the home. Federal law only requires that the sibling have an *equity interest* in the property. An equity interest could be joint ownership or a Tenancy In Common or a Remainder Interest in the homestead. An Elder Law attorney will be able to suggest a method of transferring an equity interest to the sibling that will result in a Penalty Period of a year or less. The attorney will also assist with preparing documentation to present to the DFCS to verify that:

    ⇨   the sibling owns an equity interest in the home

    ⇨   the Penalty Period for the transfer has passed

    ⇨   the sibling occupied the home for a year prior to the Applicant entering the nursing home.

A similar law applies to the Medicaid recipient who owns his home and wants to transfer it to his child. The federal law allows a transfer of the homestead to the child without penalty, provided the child lived with and took care of his parent for at least two years before the parent entered the nursing home (MA II/2342-3).

There is no requirement that the child own an equity interest in the property; but the federal statute does require that the state verify that the child lived in the home and provided care to the parent for the two years; and that this care enabled the parent to remain at home rather than be placed in a nursing home (42 U.S.C. 1396p(c)(2)(A)(iv)).

If the value of the house is not greater than the two year Penalty Period it may be just as easy to transfer the home to the child and wait out the two years. Specifically, a transfer of $100,015.92 will result in a two year penalty period: $4,167.33 x 24 = $100,015.92

If the parent's equity in the home is worth no more than $100,015.92, the home can be transferred to the child without the need for the child to prove to DHFS that care was given to the parent over that two year period.

If the home is worth significantly more, then it is important to consult with an Elder Law attorney, preferably prior to the two year period. The attorney will explain how to document that care over the two year period so that the information can be presented to the DFCS when the parent applies for Medicaid.

Some of the things the DFCS will want to know are:

⇨ the Applicant's medical condition during the two year period

⇨ whether the child lived in the home for the required period of time

⇨ what care was provided by the child that enabled the parent to remain at home

⇨ how many hours per day were spent by the child in caring for his parent

⇨ whether the child worked outside of the home during the two year period; and if so, who cared for the parent while the child was at work.

The DFCS may want a friend or family member to verify that the child did provide the necessary care during the two years. Once it is established by the DFCS that state and federal requirements are satisfied, the property can be transferred to the child without affecting the right of the Applicant to receive Medicaid benefits (MA II/2342-3).

TRANSFERS TO A DISABLED CHILD

In Georgia, the Applicant or his spouse may transfer any of their Resources to a child (minor or adult) who is blind, or disabled without penalty (42 U.S.C. 1396p(c)(2A), MA II/2342-3). In the event that the child does not have a determination of blindness or disability from the Social Security Administration, the DFCS will review the child's medical records to determine whether the child is blind or disabled. If the child is receiving Social Security disability benefits, the parent can transfer their home or other assets to a Community Trust for the child (see page 134).

This transfer will not disqualify the child (or the parent) from receiving government benefits, provided the Trust is drafted according to state and federal law.

CAUTION   DON'T TRY THIS ON YOUR OWN

A Medicaid Qualifying Plan is not something to attempt on your own. The Medicaid program is complex and volatile. There are many levels of law that govern Medicaid. There are the federal statutes (Social Security Act Title XIX/P.L. 89-97); the U.S. Code of Federal Regulations (42 CFR 430-435) and the Centers for Medicare and Medicaid Services State Medicaid Manual, Part 3 that say how the federal statutes are to be administered in the United States.

There are the Georgia Medicaid statutes (Title 4, Article 7 Medical Assistance); and the Georgia Rules and Regulations (Chapter 111-3-8 Rules of the Department of Community Health Medical Assistance and Chapter 350 Rules of the Department of Medical Assistance) that say how the Medicaid program is to be administered in this state. These five different sets of laws and regulations are constantly changing — often with little or no notice to the general public.

And the laws are not well written.
In *Rehabilitation Association of Virginia v. Kozlowski*, 42 F.3d 1444, 1450 (4th Cir 1994), the Court had nothing but sympathy for officials who must interpret or administer these laws. "There can be no doubt but that the statutes and provisions in question, involving the financing of Medicare and Medicaid, are among the most completely impenetrable texts within human experience. Indeed, one approaches them . . . with dread, for not only are they dense reading of the most tortuous kind, but Congress also revisits the area frequently, generously cutting and pruning in the process and making any solid grasp of the matters addressed merely a passing phase."

Judges in the federal District Court were equally critical: "The Social Security Act is among the most intricate ever drafted by Congress. Its Byzantine construction ... makes the Act 'almost unintelligible to the uninitiated.' ... The District Court ... described the Medicaid statute as 'an aggravated assault on the English language, resistant to attempts to understand it'." (*Schweiker v. Gray Panthers*, 453 U.S. 34(1981)).

Most states have a manual that they provide to workers who are in charge of implementing the Medicaid Program. In Georgia, that manual is Volume II of the MEDICAL ASSISTANCE MANUAL. The Manual explains how eligibility is to be determined when an Applicant applies.

Even with the Manual available to the workers, there is variation in the way the law is applied. A Medicaid qualifying option may be accepted in one county and challenged in another. If DFCS decides to challenge a particular strategy, even though that strategy is based on federal or state law, you will have no choice but to appeal the ruling.

THE MEDICAID APPEAL

An Applicant who is denied Medicaid benefits will receive notice from the Division of Family and Children Services ("DFCS") that he has the right to appeal. The first step in the appeal process is for the Applicant, or someone acting on his behalf, to submit a written request for a hearing. Once requested, the Commissioner of Medical Assistance will appoint an Administrative Law Judge to conduct the hearing. The Administrative Law Judge is an attorney who has a working knowledge of the Georgia Medicaid program and who has not been involved in the case prior to the hearing.

The hearing is conducted at one of the offices of the Department of Community Health. The Administrative Law Judge will set the time and place of the hearing. Before the hearing, he will settle issues that are raised relating to the discovery of evidence to be presented at the hearing. For example, he will determine whether it is necessary to take the testimony of a witness by deposition instead of requiring the person to appear at the hearing.

At the hearing, the Administrative Law Judge will take oaths, hear testimony and then decide the facts of the case (Georgia Rules and Regulations ("GRR") 350-1-.01, 350-4-.08, 350-4-.13, 350-4-.18).

The hearing is a complex legal proceeding. The Department of Community Health will present evidence and quote laws that supports their ruling. The rules of evidence used at the hearing are the same as are used in the Superior Court for civil matters (GRR 350-4-.20). To win the appeal, the Applicant (or his family member) will need to know how to discover and present that evidence to prove their case.

Few Applicants (or their family members) have the necessary knowledge and skills to adequately represent their side of the argument, so it is important to employ an attorney who is familiar with the Medicaid law and skilled at presenting evidence that will support the position of the Applicant. Those who cannot afford to employ an attorney, should ask Legal Services for assistance. See page xiii for information about how to locate the Legal Services office nearest you.

The Administrative Law Judge will compile an Official Record of the hearing, including all of the filings, motions, intermediate rulings and evidence presented at the hearing. He will base his decision on the Official Record and forward his decision to the Department of Community Health within 30 days. The Department will send a copy of the decision to DFCS and to the Applicant, together with a notice that they have 5 days to ask the Commission to review the decision of the Administrative Law Judge. If anyone requests a transcript of the record, that party will have an additional 5 days to appeal (GRR 350-4-.27, 35-4-.28, 350-4-.29).

The final decision by the Commissioner will be made within 30 days after his receipt of the request for review. If the Commissioner fails to give his decision, that means he agrees with the ruling of the Administrative Law Judge (OCG 49-4-153).

If the Applicant loses at this Administrative level, he can appeal to Georgia Superior Court to review the case. If the Applicant is turned down in Superior Court, he can appeal to a federal court — all the way up to the United States Supreme Court.

As you can see, appealing the decision of the DFCS is complicated, and time consuming. It is important to employ an attorney to help with the appeal and that can be expensive.

In Chapter 10 we presented many different options that are legally available to the Applicant at this time. The goal is to get the Applicant qualified for Medicaid as quickly as possible, and with the least amount of hassle. It is better to choose a strategy that has been allowed in the past, rather than chance a denial of the application and be forced to appeal the decision.

An experienced Elder Law attorney can explain what strategies have been allowed in the past in your county and which strategies are likely to be challenged. The key word is "experienced." Before employing an attorney, determine what percentage of his practice is devoted to Medicaid eligibility; how long he has practiced Elder Law in that county; and whether he is familiar with the appeals process, should the need arise.

Guiding Those You Love 12

Once you are satisfied with your Estate Plan, then the final thing to consider is whether your heirs will be able to locate your assets after you're gone.

Most people have their business records in one place, their Will in another place, car titles and deeds in still another place. When someone dies, their beneficiaries may feel as if they are playing a game of "hide and seek" with the decedent. The game might be fun were it not for the fact that unlocated items may be forever lost. For example, suppose you die in an accident and no one knows you are insured by your credit card company for accidental death in the amount of $25,000. The only one to profit is the insurance company, which is just that much richer because no one told them that you died as a result of an accident.

And how about a key to a safe deposit box? Will anyone find it? Even if they find the key, how will they locate the box?

It is not difficult to arrange things so that your affairs are always in order. It amounts to being aware of what you own (and owe) and keeping a record of your possessions. A side benefit is that by doing so, you will always know where all your business records are. If you ever spent time trying to collect information to file your taxes or trying to find a lost stock or bond certificate, you will appreciate the value of organizing your records.

POINTING THE WAY

Heirs need all the help they can get. It is difficult enough dealing with the loss, without the frustration of trying to locate important documents. Your heirs will have no problem locating your assets if you keep all of your records in a single place. It can be a desk drawer or a file cabinet or even a shoe box. It is helpful if you keep a separate file or folder for each type of investment. You might consider setting up the following folders:

THE BANK & SECURITIES FOLDER

Store your original certificates for stocks, bonds, mutual funds, certificates of deposit, in a folder labeled **BANK & SECURITIES FOLDER**. In addition to the original certificate include a copy of the contract you signed with each financial institution. The contract will show where you have funds and who you named as beneficiary or joint owner of the account. If someone owes you money and has signed a promissory note or mortgage that identifies you as the lender, then you can store these documents in this folder as well.

If you have a safe deposit box, keep a record of its location and the number of the box, in this folder. Keep a copy of all of the items stored in the box in this folder. If you have an extra key to the box, put it in this folder.

E-bank Accounts

If you are doing your banking on-line, it is important to leave a record of your passwords so that your family can access the account in the event of your incapacity or death. The same applies if you have on-line brokerage or installment loan accounts. Keep a paper record of these accounts in your Bank & Securities Folder.

🗁 THE INSURANCE FOLDER

The INSURANCE FOLDER is for each insurance policy that you own, be it life insurance, car insurance, homeowner's insurance or a health care insurance. If you purchased real property, you may have received a title commitment at closing and the original title insurance policy some weeks later when you received your original deed from recording. If you cannot locate the title insurance policy, then contact the closing agent and have them send you a copy of your title insurance policy.

🗁 THE PENSION AND ANNUITY FOLDER

Put all of the documents relating to your pension or annuity in this folder. Include the telephone number and/or address of the person to contact in the event of your death.

FOR FEDERAL RETIREES

If you are a Federal Retiree, you should have received your PERSONAL IDENTIFICATION NUMBER (PIN) and the person who will inherit your pension (your *survivor annuitant*) should have received his/her own PIN as well. It is relatively simple to obtain this during your lifetime, but it may be difficult and/or stressful for your survivor annuitant to work through the system once you are gone.

Survivor annuitant benefits are not automatic. Your survivor annuitant must apply for them by submitting a death claim to the Office of Personnel Management. Your survivor needs to know that it is necessary to apply and also how to apply. You can call the Office of Personnel Management at (888) 767-6738 to get printed information that you can keep in this folder to guide your survivor annuitant through the process. You can also download information from their Web site: http://www.opm.gov

A Will Is Not Enough In Georgia

🗁   THE DEED FOLDER

Place the original deed (or a copy if the original is in a safe deposit box) in a separate DEED FOLDER. Include cemetery deeds, condominium deeds, timesharing certificates, deed to out of state property, etc. Also include a copy of related documents such as an Abstract of Title, or a recorded condominium approval. If you have a title insurance policy, put the original in the insurance folder, and a copy in this folder. If you own several properties, you may want to have a separate folder for each property which includes all of the closing documents for that parcel of land.

If you have a mortgage on your property, put a copy of the recorded mortgage and promissory note in a separate LIABILITY FOLDER. Once the mortgage is paid off, the lender should give you Satisfaction of Mortgage. The Satisfaction needs to be recorded. Keep the recorded Satisfaction together with the deed to the property. Remember to remove the paid mortgage from your Liability Folder

LOCATING REAL PROPERTY

If you own a vacant lot, your beneficiaries will find the deed (or a copy) in this folder but that deed will not contain the address of that property because it doesn't have one. The post office does not assign a street address until there is a building on the site. Your beneficiary could get the location of the property from city or county records. But why make things hard for them? Include a simple handwritten note in this folder that tells them exactly how to locate the property.

📁 THE TAX RECORD FOLDER

Your Personal Representative (or next of kin) will need to file your final income tax returns. Keep a copy of your tax returns (both federal and state) for the past three years in your Tax Record Folder. As explained in Chapter 3, beginning in 2010, there will be a cap on the step-up basis to 4.3 million dollars for property inherited by your spouse and 1.3 million for property inherited by anyone else. It is important to keep a record of the basis of your property, not only for your heirs, but for yourself should you decide to sell the property during your lifetime. If you purchase real property, you need to keep a record of the purchase price as well as monies you paid to improve the property. You need these records to determine whether a Capital Gains Tax is due on the transfer. Your accountant can help you set up a bookkeeping system to keep a running record of your basis in everything you own of value.

📁 THE LIABILITY FOLDER

The LIABILITY FOLDER should contain all loan documents of debts that you owe. For example, if you purchased real property and have a mortgage on that property, put a copy of the mortgage and promissory note in this folder. If you owe money on a car, put the loan documents here. A lease is a liability, because you have contracted to pay a certain amount for the period of the lease, so include a copy of any lease agreement in this Liability Folder. If you have a credit card, put a copy of the contract you signed with the credit card company in this folder.

By having a record of your assets and outstanding debts, you can calculate your net worth (what you own less what you owe) whenever you wish.

A Will Is Not Enough In Georgia

🗀 THE PERSONAL PROPERTY FOLDER

MOTOR VEHICLES

Put all motor vehicle titles in a Personal Property Folder. This includes cars, mobile homes, boats, planes, etc. If you owe money on the vehicle, the lender may have possession of the title certificate. If such is the case, then put a copy of the title certificate and registration in this folder and a copy of the loan documents in a separate liability folder. If you own a boat or plane, then identify the location of the motor vehicle. For example, if you are leasing space in an airplane hangar or in a marina, keep a copy of the leasing agreement in this folder.

JEWELRY

If you own expensive jewelry, keep a picture of the item together with the sales receipt or written appraisal in this folder.

COLLECTOR'S ITEMS

If you own a valuable art or coin collection, or any other item of significant value, include a picture of the item in this folder. Also include evidence of ownership of the item, such as a sales receipt or a certificate of authenticity, or a written appraisal of the property.

🗀 THE PERSONAL RECORDS FOLDER

The PERSONAL RECORDS FOLDER should include documents that relate to you personally, such as a birth certificate, naturalization papers, marriage certificate, divorce papers, military records, Social Security card; etc.

🗁 THE ESTATE PLANNING DOCUMENT FOLDER

WILL/TRUST

Place your Will and/or Trust in a separate folder. If the original document is in a safe deposit box, place a copy of the document in this folder together with instructions about how to find the original. Georgia residents can file their Will in the office of the judge of the Probate Court (OCG 15-9-38). If you placed your Will with the Probate Court, put the Court receipt for the document in this folder.

It is important to keep a copy of your Will or Trust because over the years you may forget what provision you made. Keeping a copy in your home may save you the time and effort to retrieve the document, just to determine whether it needs to be updated.

PRENUPTIAL/POSTNUPTIAL AGREEMENT

Prenuptial or postnuptial agreements usually provide for the disposition of your property upon your death, so a copy of the agreement should be included in this folder.

OTHER ESTATE PLANNING DOCUMENTS

You can include the original or a copy of other Estate Planning Documents in this folder such as your:
- ⇨ Financial Power of Attorney
- ⇨ Durable Power of Attorney for Health Care
- ⇨ Living Will
- ⇨ Preneed Funeral Contract.

THE QUICK-FIND FOLDER

Many do not have the time, nor inclination, to "play" with all these folders. They do not anticipate an immediate demise. Getting hit by a truck, or dying in a fiery plane crash is not something to think about, much less prepare for. But consider that death is not the only problem. You could take suddenly ill (say with a stroke) and become incapacitated. Even the most time-starved optimist should have a murmur of concern that his loved ones will be left with a mess should something unforeseen happen.

If you do not feel like doing a complete job of organizing your records at this time, consider an abridged version. You can set up a single folder and place all of your important papers in that folder. You need to make the folder easily accessible to whoever you wish to manage your affairs in the event of your incapacity or death. You can do this by letting that person know of the existence of the folder and how to get it in an emergency.

You can keep the folder in an easily accessed place in your home with the folder identified as containing important papers. We labeled it "THE QUICK-FIND FOLDER" because the folder gives you and your family easy access to important information and/or documents. But you can create your own heading such as: "MY IMPORTANT PAPERS" or if you want a particular person to access the folder, you might label it: "RECORDS FOR MY SON, ROBERT"

It is helpful if you include a list of all you own and the location of each item in that folder.

We discussed people's natural disinclination to make an Estate Plan until they are faced with their own mortality. Many believe that they will make just one Will and then die (maybe that's why they put off making a Will). The reality is, most people who make a Will, change it at least once before they die. If you have an Estate Plan, it is important to update it when any of the following events take place:

✍ CHANGE IN MARITAL STATUS

If you marry or divorce, there are certain changes that take place by law. For example, if you appointed someone to be your Health Care Agent, then unless your Health Care Power of Attorney provides otherwise, once you marry that nomination is revoked. After the date of the marriage, you can appoint your spouse or anyone else you choose to serve as your Health Care Agent.

Similarly, if you appointed your spouse as your Health Care Agent, should you divorce or have your marriage annulled, your former spouse will have no authority to make your health care decisions (OCG 31-36-6).

Should you divorce and die before you get around to changing your Will, any provision that you made for your former spouse in the document will be read as if he/she died before you (OCG 53-4-49).

But it is important to not just rely on the law. Best to change all documents after a divorce or separation. This includes deeds, pension plans, insurance policies, etc.

NOTIFY EMPLOYER OF CHANGE

If you change your marital status (marry or divorce) you need to tell your employer of the change so that the employer can change your status for purposes of paycheck tax deductions. If you have a health insurance plan or a pension plan that provides benefits to your spouse, these need to be changed as well.

Under Georgia law an employer can pay up to $2,500 of monies owed to a deceased employee (wages, vacation pay, other company benefits) to anyone chosen by the employee. If you named someone to receive these funds, and then marry or divorce, you need to update your work file and name the beneficiary who is to receive these funds should you die. If you neglect to name someone, your employer can give the funds to your surviving spouse. If you are single, but have a minor child, the monies can be given to the child's Guardian. In the absence of a named beneficiary, or a surviving spouse or minor child, the wages will become part of your Probate Estate, to be distributed according to Georgia law (OCG 34-7-4).

✍ A CHANGE IN RELATIONSHIP

Getting married, separated or divorced; having a child; having a beneficiary of your Estate die, are all profound changes in one's life. When the dust settles, it is important to examine your Estate Plan to see if it needs revision. If you have a Trust, you can change it by having your attorney prepare an *amendment* to the Trust. If you have a Will, your attorney can prepare a *codicil* (a supplement) to the Will. It is important to have changes made by a properly drafted and signed document. If you make changes by crossing things out or writing over your Will, or Trust, the validity of the document can be challenged once you die.

If you simply rip up the old Will, that will effectively revoke the Will (OCG 53-4-42, 53-4-44). But it could happen that someone (perhaps your attorney) has a copy of the Will. If no one knows that you revoked the Will, they may think the Will is lost and then offer the copy of the Will for Probate. If you draft a new Will, the first paragraph should say, "I revoke all prior Wills ..." This makes it clear that you want the new Will to replace all other Wills.

 ### NEW SPOUSE OR CHILD CAN CHALLENGE OLD WILL

If you marry and "forget" to change the Will you prepared prior to your marriage, your spouse can challenge your Will unless she gave up her rights in a prenuptial or other marital agreement, or unless you included a provision in your Will indicating that you intended your Will to be effective after your marriage. Without such agreement or indication, your spouse is entitled to inherit as much as he/she would have inherited had you died without a Will.

The same applies to a child born or adopted after you prepared your Will. If you had children when you prepared your Will and you made a gift in your Will to your children, then even though you did not include the name of the afterborn child in that gift, the afterborn is entitled to share the gift equally with his/her siblings. If you made no provision for any of your children in your Will, and you have a child later on, under Georgia law, your child is entitled to inherit as much as the child would have inherited had you died without a Will (OCG 53-4-48).

BENEFICIARY MOVES OR DIES

Most people remember to name an alternate beneficiary should one of their beneficiaries die. But how many of us remember to notify the pension plan or insurance company when a beneficiary moves?

It is important that your beneficiary's address be available to those in charge of distributing funds upon your death. Many life insurance proceeds are never paid because the company cannot locate the beneficiary. The Actuarial Office of the Federal Employees' Group Life Insurance Program reported that as of September, 2003, they had over 55.8 million dollars in unpaid benefits, mostly because they could not locate the beneficiary at the last given address.

RELOCATION TO A NEW STATE OR COUNTRY

There is no need to change your Estate Plan for a move within the state of Georgia. There is much to check out if you are moving to another state. If you remain in Georgia and you deposited your Will with the Probate Court, you need to retrieve your Will and deposit it in the Probate Court of the county of your new residence (OCG 15-9-38). If you are leaving the state, you need to retrieve your Will and take it with you. Not all states allow a Will to be deposited with the Court prior to the death of the Will maker. You may need to make other arrangements for the storage of your Will in the new state.

If your attorney has your original Will or any other original of your Estate Planning documents, then unless you plan to continue to employ him, you need to retrieve these items to take with you to the new state.

You need to determine whether your Will conforms to the laws of the state of your new residence. Most states will honor a Will drafted according to Georgia law, however, the rights of a spouse vary considerably state to state. If you are married and have not provided the minimum amount as required by the laws of the new state, then should you die before your spouse, your Will may be challenged on that basis. The same applies to a Trust. Many states allow a surviving spouse to demand funds from the Trust of the decedent spouse, if the deceased spouse did not provide the minimum amount to his spouse as required by the laws of that state.

LAWS OF DESCENT

If you do not have a Will, then it is important to check out the Laws of Descent and Distribution for that state. In some states they are referred to as the *Laws of Intestate Succession*. Each state has its own laws relating to the inheritance of property and those laws are very different from each other. Who has the right to inherit your property in the state of Georgia may be different from who has the right to inherit your property in another state. If you do not have a Will, then this is the time to think about who will get your property in the state of your new residence.

This is especially important for those who are married. The right of a spouse to inherit property varies significantly state to state. There is a world of difference between the rights of a spouse in a community property state (Arizona, California, Idaho, Louisiana, Nevada, New Mexico, Texas, Washington and Wisconsin) and other states. There is even variation in the rights of a spouse from one community property state to another!

A Will Is Not Enough In Georgia

TAX CONSIDERATIONS

You need to check out the taxes of the new state. Each state has its own tax structure. Some states have an inheritance tax, or a transfer tax on all inherited property. If state taxes are high, you may need an Estate Plan that will minimize the impact of those taxes.

CREDITOR PROTECTION

Creditor protection is another item that is significantly different state to state. If you have much debt, determine what items can be inherited by your family free of your debts in that state.

OTHER ESTATE PLANNING DOCUMENTS

Many states have laws directing physicians to honor a Medical Directive that is properly drafted in another state. Some states will not recognize a Directive for Health Care unless it is drafted according to the laws of that state. But even if the laws of the state honor your Georgia Durable Power of Attorney for Health Care, consider drafting another in the new state. Medical Directives vary significantly state to state. Other states may have laws that enable you to appoint someone with powers similar to your Health Care Agent, but the laws of the state may refer to such person as a *Patient Advocate* or a *Health Care Surrogate* or a *Health Care Representative.*

It is best to sign a new Power of Attorney For Health Care using the form and terminology recognized in the new state, rather than chance any confusion should you become ill and find yourself in an emergency situation. Similarly, if you have appointed someone to handle your finances under a Financial Power of Attorney, you may want to have another prepared in conformity with the laws of the new state, so there will be no question of the right of your Attorney-In-Fact to conduct business on your behalf.

RELOCATING THE MEDICAID RECIPIENT

If your family member is a Medicaid Recipient, and you want to move him to another state, you need to check out whether he will continue to be eligible for Medicaid in that state. As explained in the previous chapter, Medicaid is both a state and federal program. Once a person qualifies for Medicaid in one state, he can be transferred to another state; provided he qualifies under that state's Medical Assistance Program.

But qualification for Medical Assistance varies significantly state to state. For example, a Medicaid Annuity is allowed as a spend-down option in the state of Georgia, however, some other states do not allow this strategy, and might count the purchase as an impermissible transfer of funds. If you plan to move a Medicaid Recipient to another state, it is important to first check with an Elder Law attorney in that state. He will explain the Medicaid eligibility laws of the state to you. He will be able to tell you can be done in order to have the Recipient qualify for Medicaid in his state.

As you can see, state law has an important impact on your Estate Plan. When moving to another state, it is important to either educate yourself about the laws of the state, or to consult with an attorney who can assist you in reviewing your Estate Plan to see whether your current plan will accomplish your goals in that state.

A Will Is Not Enough In Georgia

✍ A SIGNIFICANT CHANGE IN THE LAW

We pay our legislators (state and federal) to make laws and, if necessary, change those in effect. We pay judges to interpret the law and that interpretation may change the way the law operates. The legislature and the judiciary do their job and so laws change frequently. Tax laws are particularly volatile. The 2001 change in the Federal Estate Tax law gradually increases the Exclusion amount so that by 2010 no Federal Estate Tax will be due regardless of the value of your Estate. You may be thinking that there is no need for an Estate Tax plan because you don't intend to die prior to 2010. But any certainty relating to death and taxes is false security (especially taxes, in this case). As explained in Chapter 3, the law as passed in 2001, is effective only until December 31, 2010. If lawmakers do nothing, then on January 1, 2011, the Federal Estate Tax goes back into effect; and Estates that exceed one million dollars will once again be subject to Estate Taxes.

And that is not the only uncertainty. Each state has its own Estate Tax structure. It remains to be seen how each state will react to the position taken by the federal government in 2010. If federal Estate Taxes are phased out altogether, some states may follow the lead of the federal government and dispense with Estate Taxes. However, with states struggling to balance the budget, more likely they will see this as an opportunity to increase their Estate Taxes, so that Estate Taxes that would have been paid to the federal government will now be paid to the state.

You need to keep up with the news to learn about changes in the law that affect your Estate Plan. It is a good idea to check with your attorney on a regular basis to see if any change in the state or federal law affects your current Estate plan. And also check out the Eagle Publishing Company Web site for changes we will post to keep this book fresh. **http://www.eaglepublishing.com**

Used to be, that housewives did a once a year, floor to ceiling, "spring housecleaning." We know of no survey telling whether today's houseperson conducts an annual purge of dirt and clutter. We suspect it went by the wayside when housewives entered the work force as full time employees. But it was a good practice. In many cases, it was the only time of the year when the house was truly clean and tidy.

It is a good idea to incorporate that old-fashioned house-cleaning practice to your financial records and clean them up on a regular basis. There is no need to keep the deed to real property that you have long since sold; a lease agreement to an apartment you no longer rent; a credit card to a closed account, etc.

Many hesitate to toss out some scrap of paper for fear it will not be available for future reference. There are documents you may need to keep for a lengthy period of time to establish a basis for tax purposes. You can avoid the problem of keeping too much, or not enough, by taking your box (or folder) of records with you the next time you visit with your accountant or attorney. You can ask your advisor to help you organize your records and assist with your "housecleaning."

Keys are another item to keep up to date. You may have a sentimental reason to keep old keys, but there is no business reason to keep a key to a car you no longer own, a safe deposit box you no longer lease, etc. Keeping such keys can only cause confusion should you become disabled or die. Whoever takes possession of your property will be left with mysterious keys. He will probably think the keys are protecting something of value.

Unless you enjoy picturing an heir's frustration as he seeks an imaginary treasure, pitch the key.

Glossary

ABSTRACT OF TITLE An *Abstract of Title* is a condensed history of the title to the land. It consists of a summary of recorded documents that affect the land, including mortgages.

ACTUARIAL TABLE An *actuarial table* is a table organized according to statistical data that indicates the life expectancy of a person.

ADMINISTRATION The *administration* of a Probate Estate is the management and settlement of the decedent's affairs. There are different types of administration. See ANCILLARY ADMINISTRATION.

ADMINISTRATIVE LAW JUDGE An *Administrative Law Judge* is someone who is appointed to conduct an administrative hearing. He has the power to administer oaths, take testimony, and then decide the facts of the case. Although he can decide the facts of the case, the final outcome of the hearing is decided by the government agency that appointed the Administrative Law Judge.

ADMINISTRATIVE CODE   The *Administrative Code* is the set of rules used by governmental agencies to apply laws enacted by the legislature. The Administrative Code interprets the law and describes the agency's requirements to implement that law. See *CFR*.

AFFIANT   An *Affiant* is someone who signs an affidavit and swears or acknowledges that it is true in the presence of a notary public or other person with authority to administer an oath or take acknowledgments.

AFFIDAVIT An *Affidavit* is a written statement of fact made by someone voluntarily, under oath, or acknowledged as being true, in the presence of a notary public or someone else who has authority to administer an oath or take acknowledgments.

AGENT An *Agent* is someone who is authorized by another (the principal) to act for or in place of the principal.

AGENCY ACCOUNT An *Agency account* is a bank account in which the owner of the funds in the account authorizes another to make bank transactions as his Agent under a Power of Attorney.

AMENDMENT An *amendment* to a Trust is an addition to the Trust that changes the provisions of the Trust.

ANATOMICAL GIFT An *anatomical gift* is the donation of all or part of the body of the decedent for a specified purpose, such as transplantation or research.

ANCILLARY ADMINISTRATION An *Ancillary Administration* is a Probate procedure that aids or assists the original (primary) Probate proceeding. Ancillary administration is conducted to determine the beneficiary of the decedent's property located within that state, and to determine whether the property is taxable in that state.

ANNUAL GIFT TAX EXCLUSION The *Annual Gift Tax Exclusion* is the amount a person can gift to another each year without being required to file a federal Gift Tax Return. The Annual Gift Tax Exclusion is currently $11,000.

ANNUITANT An *Annuitant* is someone who is entitled to receive payments under an annuity contract.

ANNUITY CONTRACT An *annuity contract* is a contract that gives someone (the annuitant) the right to receive periodic payments (monthly, quarterly) for the life of the annuitant or for a given number of years.

ASSET An *asset* is anything owned by someone that has a value, including personal property (jewelry, paintings, securities, cash, motor vehicles, etc.) and real property (condominiums, vacant lots, acreage, residences, etc.).

ASSIGN To *assign* is to transfer one's rights to another; e.g. a person who has the right to receive income from a partnership may assign that right to another person,

ATTORNEY or ATTORNEY AT LAW An *attorney*, also known as an *Attorney at law*, or a *lawyer*, is someone who is licensed by the state to practice law in that state.

ATTORNEY-IN-FACT An *Attorney-In-Fact* is someone appointed to act as an Agent for another (the Principal) under a Power of Attorney.

BASIS The *basis* is a value that is assigned to an asset for the purpose of determining the gain (or loss) on the sale of the item or in determining the value of the item in the hands of someone who has received it as a gift.

BENEFICIARY A *beneficiary* is one who benefits from the act of another or from the transfer of property. In this book we refer to a beneficiary as someone named in a Will, Trust, or deed to receive property, or someone who inherits property under the Laws of Intestate Succession.

BENEFICIARY ACCOUNT A *beneficiary account* is a bank account with a named beneficiary. The owner of the funds in the account directs the bank to give the funds remaining in the account to the named beneficiary upon the death of all of the owners of the bank account. *Pay On Death* and *In Trust For* accounts are beneficiary accounts.

BONA FIDE A *bona fide* act is something that is done in good faith; honestly, openly and without deceit or fraud.

BURDEN OF PROOF The *burden of proof* is the duty of one of the parties in a dispute to establish the facts in the case. Who has the burden of proof is established by law.

BY REPRESENTATION *By representation* is a method of distributing property to a group of people such that if one of them dies before the gift is made, then the deceased person's share goes to his/her descendants.

CAPITAL GAINS TAX A *Capital Gains Tax* is a tax on the increase in the basis of property sold by a taxpayer.

CASH SURRENDER VALUE The *Cash Surrender Value* of a life insurance policy is the amount of money the insurance company will pay to the owner of an insurance policy in the event the owner cancels the policy before the death of the person who is insured under the policy.

CFR The *Code of Federal Regulations ("CFR")* is the annual cumulation of regulations set by federal executive agencies combined with previous regulations that are still in effect. The CFR contains the general body of laws that govern the practices and procedures of federal administrative agencies.

CHARITABLE REMAINDER ANNUITY TRUST   A *Charitable Remainder Annuity Trust* is a Trust that pays an annuity to a designated person (the Annuitant) for a certain period of time or until his death. Once the annuity is paid, whatever remains in the Trust is donated to a tax exempt charity.

CLAIM A *claim* against the decedent's Estate is a demand for payment. To be effective, the claim must be filed with the Probate court within the time limits set by law.

CLOSE CORPORATION A *Close Corporation* is a corporation whose voting shares are held by a single shareholder or a small, closely-knit, group of shareholders.

CODE A *Code* is a body of laws arranged systematically for easy reference e.g. the Internal Revenue Code.

CODICIL A *codicil* to a Will is an addition to the Will that changes or replaces certain parts of the Will.

COLUMBARIUM A *columbarium* is a vault with niches (spaces) for urns that contain the ashes of cremated bodies.

COMMON LAW MARRIAGE A *Common Law marriage* is one that is entered into without a state marriage license or any kind of official marriage ceremony. A Common Law marriage is created by an agreement to marry, followed by the two living together, and telling everyone they know that they are husband and wife. Georgia does not recognize a Common Law marriage unless it was entered into in another state that considers the union to be a valid marriage.

COMMUNITY PROPERTY   Certain states (Arizona, California, Idaho, Louisiana, Nevada, New Mexico, Texas, Washington, and Wisconsin) have laws stating that property acquired by husband or wife, or both, during their marriage is *Community Property* and is owned equally by both of them.

COMMUNITY TRUST A *Community Trust* is a Trust established according to Georgia law to provide for the supplemental needs of a disabled person; i.e., items such as clothing, entertainment, hobbies, etc. that are not supplied to the disabled person under Medicaid or other medical assistance programs.

CONFLICT OF INTEREST A *conflict of interest* is a conflict between the official duties of a fiduciary (guardian, Trustee, attorney, etc.) and his own private interest. For example, it is a conflict of interest for a Successor Trustee to use Trust property for his own personal profit.

CONSERVATOR   A *Conservator* is someone appointed by the Probate Court to manage, protect and preserve the property of someone who is missing, or who the Court finds is unable to care for his property because of age (a minor) or incapacity.

CORPORATION   A *Corporation* is a company created by one or more persons according to the laws of the state. The company is owned by the *shareholders* or *stockholders*. Each owner has limited liability (see Limited Liability).

COURT The *Court* as used in this book is the Court that handles Probate matters. When referring to an order made by the Court, the term is synonymous with "judge," i.e., an "order of the Court" is an order made by the judge of the Court.

CREDITOR A *creditor* is someone to whom a debt is owed by another person (the *debtor*).

CURTESY *Curtesy* is the right of a husband, upon the death of his wife, to a life estate in real property she owned during their marriage, provided they had a surviving child who could inherit the property. This English Common Law has been abolished in most states, including Georgia.

CUSTODIAN A *Custodian* under the *Georgia Uniform Gifts to Minors Act* is a financial institution or person who accepts responsibility for the care and management of property given to a minor child.

DAMAGES *Damages* is money that is awarded by a Court as compensation to someone who has been injured by the action of another.

DEBTOR A *debtor* is someone who owes payment of money or services to another person (the *creditor*).

DECEDENT The *decedent* is the person who died.

DECLARANT The *Declarant* is the person who signs an *Advance Directive For Health Care* in accordance with Georgia law.

DESCENDANT A *descendant* is someone who descends from a common ancestor. There are two kinds of descendants: a *lineal descendant* and a *collateral descendant*. The lineal descendant is one who descends in a straight line such as father to son to grandson. The collateral descendant is one who descends in a parallel line, such as a cousin. In this book, unless otherwise stated, the term *descendant* refers to a *lineal descendant*.

DFCS A *Division of Family and Children Services ("DFCS")* is the branch of the Georgia *Department of Human Resources* that is responsible to implement the Medicaid program. The DFCS takes applications and determines whether the Applicant is qualified to receive Medical Assistance in the state of Georgia.

DISTRIBUTION The *distribution* of a Trust or Probate Estate is the giving to the beneficiary that part of the Estate to which the beneficiary is entitled.

DOWER *Dower* is the right of a wife, upon the death of her husband, to a Life Estate in one-third of all real property that he owned during their marriage. This English Common Law has been abolished in most states, including Georgia.

DURABLE As used in the Power of Attorney, the word *durable* means that the Power of Attorney will remain in effect in the event that the principal (the person giving the Power of Attorney) becomes incapacitated.

DURABLE POWER OF ATTORNEY FOR HEALTH CARE A *Durable Power of Attorney for Health Care* is a document in which someone (the *Principal*) gives another (his *Health Care Agent*) authority to make medical decisions on behalf of the Principal.

ENTITLEMENT An *entitlement* is a legal right to receive a benefit of income, property or services.

EQUITY The *equity* in a home is the market value of the home less monies owed on the property (mortgages, tax liens, etc.)

EQUITY INTEREST   An *equity interest* is an ownership interest. It is the value of the ownership interest over and above monies owed on the property.

ESCROW ACCOUNT An *Escrow Account* is a bank account held in the name of a depositor and an Escrow Agent. The monies in the account are returnable to the depositor or to another party upon fulfillment of a condition. For example, a person may put a deposit on the purchase of a home and have an Escrow Agent hold the deposit until closing. At closing the deposit will go to the seller of the home.

ESTATE A person's *Estate* is all of the property (both real and personal property) owned by that person.   A person's Estate is also referred to as his *Taxable Estate* because all of the decedent's assets must be included when determining whether any Estate taxes are due when the person dies. Compare to *Probate Estate*.

EXECUTOR   An *Executor* (feminine *Executrix*) is a legal term found in many Wills. The term refers to the person named by the Will maker to carry out directions given in the Will. In modern Wills, that person is referred to as the *Personal Representative*.

FACE VALUE   The *face value* of a life insurance policy is the value stated on the insurance certificate or policy. It is the amount to be paid upon the death of the insured person.

FIDUCIARY A *Fiduciary* is one who takes on the duty of holding property in Trust for another or acting for the benefit of another, such as a Personal Representative, Trustee, Guardian etc.. A fiduciary relationship is also one that is developed out of trust and confidence. For example, an attorney has a fiduciary relationship with his client.

FORECLOSURE   *Foreclosure* is a court proceeding in which a lender either takes title to, or forces the sale of, property owned by the borrower, in order to satisfy the debt.

GRANTEE   The *Grantee* of a deed is the person who receives title to real property from the *Grantor*.

GRANTOR   The *Grantor* is someone who transfers property. The Grantor of a deed, is the person who transfers real property to a new owner (the Grantee). The Grantor of a Trust is someone who creates the Trust and then transfers property into the Trust. Also see *Settlor*.

GRR   *The Georgia Rules and Regulations (GRR)* is the set of rules used by governmental agencies to apply laws enacted by the Georgia legislature.

GUARANTOR   A *Guarantor* is someone who promises to pay a debt or perform a contract for another in the event that person does not fulfill his obligation.

GUARDIAN   A *Guardian* is someone who has legal authority to care for the person or property of a minor or for someone who has been found by the court to be incapacitated.

HEALTH CARE AGENT   A *Health Care Agent* is someone who is appointed by another (the *Principal*) to authorize medical treatment for the Principal, in the event the Principal is to too ill to do so himself.

HEIR   An *Heir* is anyone entitled to inherit the decedent's property under the Laws of Descent in the event that the decedent dies without a valid Will.

HOLOGRAPHIC WILL A *Holographic Will* is a Will written, dated and signed by the hand of the Will maker himself. Many states refuse to admit a Holographic Will into Probate unless it is witnessed according to the laws of the state.

HOMESTEAD The *homestead* is the dwelling that is owned, and occupied, in the state of Georgia, as the owner's principal residence.

INCAPACITATED   The term *incapacitated* is used in two ways. A person is *physically incapacitated* if he lacks the ability to perform certain tasks. A person is *legally incapacitated* if a Court finds that he is unable to care for his person or property.

INTER VIVOS TRUST   An *Inter Vivos Trust* (also known as a *Living Trust*) is a Trust that is created and becomes effective during the lifetime of the Grantor (or Settlor) as opposed to a Trust that he includes as part of his Will to take effect upon his death.

INTESTATE *Intestate* means not having a Will or dying without a Will. *Testate* is to have a Will or dying with a Will.

IRREVOCABLE CONTRACT An *irrevocable contract* is a contract that cannot be revoked, withdrawn, or cancelled by any of the parties to that contract.

IRREVOCABLE LIFE INSURANCE TRUST An *Irrevocable Life Insurance Trust* is a Trust that is set up to purchase life insurance. The proceeds of the life insurance policy can be used   to pay taxes that may be due upon the death of the insured person.

IRA ACCOUNT An *Individual Retirement Account ("IRA")* is a retirement savings account in which income taxes on certain deposits and interest to the account are deferred until the monies are withdrawn from the account.

JOINT AND SEVERAL LIABILITY If two or more people agree to be *jointly and severally liable* to pay a debt, then each individually agrees to be responsible to pay the debt, and together they all agree to pay for the debt.

JOINT TENANCY In Georgia, *Joint Tenancy* means that each tenant has rights of survivorship; i.e., should one Joint Tenant die, the surviving tenants own the property.

KEOGH PLAN A *Keogh Plan* is a retirement plan available to self-employed taxpayers. Certain tax benefits are available such as tax deductions for annual contributions to the plan. The plan is named for its author, Eugene James Keogh.

KEY MAN INSURANCE *Key man insurance* is a disability and life insurance policy designed to protect a company from economic loss in the event that an important employee of the company becomes disabled or dies.

LAWS OF DESCENT AND DISTRIBUTION The *Laws of Descent and Distribution* are the laws of the state of Georgia that determine who is to inherit the decedent's Probate Estate if the decedent died without a valid Will. In some states, these laws are called the *Laws of Intestate Succession.*

LEGALESE *Legalese* refers to the use of legal terms and confusing text used by some attorneys when drafting legal documents.

LETTERS *Letters* is a document, issued by the Probate court, giving the Personal Representative authority to take possession of and to administer the Estate of the decedent.

LIEN A *lien* is a charge against a person's property as security for a debt. The lien is evidence of the creditor's right to take the property as full or partial payment, in the event that the debtor defaults in paying the monies owed.

LIFE ESTATE A *Life Estate* interest in real property is the right to possess and receive the income from that property for so long as the holder of the Life Estate lives. A one-third Life Estate interest means the person can occupy one-third of the property or receive one-third of the income generated by that property.

LIMITED LIABILITY *Limited Liability,* as related to a corporation or other company created according to state law, means that a shareholder of the company generally is not responsible to pay the debts of the company beyond the amount that he/she invested in the company.

LIMITED LIABILITY COMPANY A *Limited Liability Company* is a company created according to the laws of the state. In Georgia, it can be organized to conduct any lawful business. All of the members of the company have limited liability.

LIMITED PARTNERSHIP A *Limited Partnership* is a partnership created according to the laws of the state. Each *Limited Partner* has limited liability. Each *General Partner* has control of the business and is personally liable for all of the debts of the company. (See Limited Liability).

LINEAL DESCENDANT See *descendant.*

LITIGATION *Litigation* is the process of carrying on a lawsuit, i.e., to sue for some right or remedy in a court of law. A Litigation Attorney is one who is experienced in conducting the law suit and in particular, going to trial.

LIVING WILL A *Living Will* is a Health Care Directive that gives instructions to the physician about whether life support systems should be withheld or withdrawn in the event that the person who signs the Living Will is terminally ill or in a persistent vegetative state and unable to speak for himself.

LOOK-BACK PERIOD The *Look-back Period* is a period of con-secutive months that can be reviewed for transfers of Resources to determine whether a period of ineligibility should be imposed for the Medicaid Applicant.

MEDICAID *Medicaid* is a medical assistance program sponsored jointly by the federal and state government to provide health care for people with low income and limited resources.

NET WORTH A person's *net worth* is the value of all of the property that he owns less what he owes.

NEXT OF KIN *Next of kin* has two meanings in law: *next of kin* refers to a person's nearest blood relation or it can refer to those people (not necessarily blood relations) who are entitled to inherit the property of a person who dies without a valid Will.

NON-PROBATE TRANSFER A *Non-Probate Transfer* is a transfer made to a beneficiary of the decedent without going through a Probate procedure. This includes transfers from a joint account, a Trust, a Pay On Death account, a Transfer On Death security, etc.

PARTNERSHIP A business *partnership* is an agreement between two or more persons to use their assets and/or services to carry on a business for profit as co-owners.

PERSONAL EFFECTS *Personal effects* is personal property that is kept for one's personal use such as clothing, jewelry, books, and other items generally found in the home.

PERSONAL PROPERTY *Personal property* is all property owned by a person that is not real property (real estate). It includes personal effects, cars, securities, bank accounts, insurance policies, etc.

PERSONAL REPRESENTATIVE The *Personal Representative* is someone appointed by the Probate Court to settle the decedent's Estate and to distribute whatever is left to the proper beneficiary.

PER STIRPES *Per Stirpes* is a method of distributing property to a group of beneficiaries in the event that one of them dies before the gift is made. The deceased person's share goes to his descendants. If he has no descendants, the surviving beneficiaries share equally in the gift.

PETITION A *Petition* is a formal written, request to a Court asking the Court to take action or issue an order on a given matter; e.g. a request to appoint a Guardian.

POSTNUPTIAL AGREEMENT A *Postnuptial agreement* is an Agreement made by a couple after marriage to decide their respective rights in case of a dissolution or the death of a spouse.

POWER OF ATTORNEY A *Power of Attorney* is a document in which someone (the *Principal*) gives another (his *Agent*) authority to do specific things on behalf of the Principal.

PRENUPTIAL AGREEMENT A *Prenuptial Agreement* is an agreement made prior to marriage whereby a couple determines how their property is to be managed during their marriage and how their property is to be divided should either die, or they later divorce.

PRINCIPAL OF A POWER OF ATTORNEY The *Principal* of a Power of Attorney is someone who gives another (his *Agent*) authority to act on his (the Principal's) behalf.

PRINCIPAL OF A TRUST The *Principal* of a Trust is the Trust property. The Trust income are the monies that are earned on the Trust Principal.

PROBABLE CAUSE *Probable cause* exists if it is reasonable to believe certain facts. Mere suspicion is not enough. For probable cause to exist, there must be more evidence for the facts than against.

PROBATE *Probate* is a Court procedure in which a Court determines the existence of a valid Will. The Decedent's Estate is settled by the Personal Representative who pays all valid claims and then distributes whatever remains to the proper beneficiary.

PROBATE ESTATE The *Probate Estate* is that part of the decedent's Estate that is subject to a Probate procedure. It includes property that the decedent owned in his name only. It does not include property that was jointly held by the decedent and someone else. It does not include property held in trust for someone.

PRO BONO The term *Pro Bono* means "for the public good." When an attorney works Pro Bono, he does so voluntarily and without pay.

REAL PROPERTY *Real property*, also known as *real estate,* is land and anything permanently attached to the land such as buildings and fences.

REMAINDER INTEREST A *Remainder Interest* in real property is the property that passes to a beneficiary at the end of the life interest i.e. the property that passes to the beneficiary once the owner of the Life Estate dies.

RESIDUARY BENEFICIARY A *residuary beneficiary* of a Will is a beneficiary who is entitled to whatever is left of the Probate Estate once the specific gifts made in the Will have been distributed and once the decedent's bills, taxes and costs of Probate have been paid. If there is more than one residuary beneficiary, then unless the Will provides differently, they all share equally in the residuary Estate.

RESOURCE A *Resource* for purposes of determining Medicaid eligibility, is an asset owned by the decedent, or his spouse, that can be converted into cash to meet their needs. Federal statute 42 U.S.C. 1382b identifies what counts (and does not count) as a Resource.

REVOCABLE TRUST   A *Revocable Trust* is a Trust which can be amended or revoked by the Grantor or Settlor during his lifetime.

REVOCABLE LIVING TRUST A *Revocable Living Trust* (also known as an *Inter Vivos Trust*) is a Revocable Trust that is created and becomes effective during the lifetime of the Grantor or Settlor.

SELF PROVED WILL A *Self Proved Will* is a Will that eliminates some of the formalities of proof in a Probate procedure. The Will is made Self Proved by an Affidavit, signed by the witnesses, in the form as required by the statute.

SETTLOR A *Settlor* or a *Trustor* is someone who creates a Trust.

SIBLING   A *sibling* is one of two or more people born of the same parents; i.e., a brother or a sister. Unless, otherwise noted, we used the term to include those who have only one parent in common; i.e. a half brother or a half sister.

SOLE PROPRIETORSHIP   A *Sole Proprietorship* is a form of business ownership in which one person owns all of the assets of the business and that person is personally liable for all of the debts of the business.

SOLEMNIZE To *solemnize* a marriage is to enter into the marriage publicly, before witnesses, in contrast to a secretive or Common Law marriage.

SPECIFIC GIFT   A *Specific Gift* is a gift of a specific item of the Will maker's Estate that is made to a named beneficiary of the Will.

SPENDTHRIFT A *Spendthrift* is someone who wastes money and/or spends lavishly.

SPENDTHRIFT TRUST A *Spendthrift Trust* is a Trust created to provide monies for the living expenses of a beneficiary, and at the same time protect the monies from being taken by the creditors of the beneficiary.

SPRINGING POWER OF ATTORNEY A *Springing Power of Attorney* is a Power of Attorney that is not operational until, and unless, the Principal is incapacitated.

STANDBY GUARDIAN A *Standby Guardian* is someone appointed by a parent to take over the care of a child in the event that the parent becomes incapacitated or dies.

STATUTE OF LIMITATION A *Statute of Limitation* is a federal or state law that sets maximum time periods for taking legal action. Once the time set out in the statute passes, no legal action can be taken.

STEPPED-UP BASIS A *stepped-up basis* is the fair market value placed on property that is purchased or inherited from another. The "step-up" refers to the increase in value from the basis of the former owner (usually what he paid for it), to the basis of the new owner (usually the market value when the transfer is made).

SUCCESSOR TRUSTEE   A *Successor Trustee* is someone who takes the place of the Trustee.

SURROGATE A *surrogate* is a substitute; someone who acts in place of another.

TENANCY BY THE ENTIRETY A *Tenancy by the Entirety* is the name of a form of ownership of real property held by a husband and wife. It is a joint tenancy with right of survivorship, modified by the common law theory that the husband and wife are one. With a joint tenancy with right of survivor, each joint tenant owns their own share of the property until death, when the surviving owner owns it 100%. With a Tenancy by the Entirety, each owns 100% of the property both before and after death.

TEFRA LIEN *TEFRA* is the abbreviation for the TAX EQUITY AND FISCAL RESPONSIBILITY ACT. It is a federal law that allows states to place a lien on real property owned by those who receive Medicaid benefits after age 55.

TENANCY IN COMMON *Tenancy In Common* is a form of ownership such that each tenant owns his/her share without any claim to that share by the other tenants. Unlike a joint tenancy, there is no right of survivorship. Once a Tenant In Common dies, his/her share belongs to the tenant's Estate and not to the remaining owners of the property.

TERM LIFE INSURANCE POLICY A *Term Life Insurance policy* insures the life of a person for a certain period of time. No insurance proceeds are paid unless the insured person dies within the given period of time. The monies paid for the policy are not refundable, so a Term Life Insurance policy has no cash surrender value.

TITLE INSURANCE *Title Insurance* is a policy issued by a title insurance company after searching title to the property. The insurance covers losses that result from a defect of title, such as unpaid taxes, or a claim of ownership of the property.

TRUST AGREEMENT A *Trust Agreement* is a document in which someone (the Grantor or Settlor) creates a Trust and appoints a Trustee to manage property placed into the Trust. The usual purpose of the Trust is to benefit persons or charities named by the Grantor as beneficiaries of the Trust.

TRUSTEE A *Trustee* is a person, or institution, who accepts the duty of managing Trust property for the benefit of another.

UNASSIGNABLE ANNUITY An *unassignable annuity* is an annuity that cannot be assigned; i.e., the annuitant's benefits cannot be transferred to another.

UNDUE INFLUENCE *Undue influence* is pressure, influence or persuasion that overpowers a person's free will or judgment, so that a person acts according to the will or purpose of the dominating party.

VOID PROVISION A *void provision* is one that is not legally enforceable. For example, if a Will provision makes a gift and the Court finds that provision to be void, then the beneficiary has no legal right to receive that gift.

WAIVER A *waiver* is the intentional and voluntary giving up of a known right.

YEAR'S SUPPORT Under Georgia law, the surviving spouse and the decedent's minor child(ren) are entitled to receive a support allowance for at least a year following the death. This allowance is called the *Year's Support*.

INDEX

D

DEBTS
Business   97, 111
Credit Card
       78-80, 83, 200, 238
Joint   78, 80
Payment of   75-80

DESCENDANTS   15-17

DEEDS   30-34, 217, 237

DISABLED CHILD   131-134, 228

DIVORCE   218, 243, 244

DOCTRINE OF NECESSARIES 76

DOMESTIC PARTNER   9

DONOR CARD   161

DOWER   34, 48

DURABLE POWER OF ATTORNEY
    166, 167, 169, 175, 176
     213, 225, 240, 247

E

ELDER LAW ATTORNEY
     134, 190, 198, 201
     214, 226, 233, 248

EQUITY INTEREST   226

ERRORS & OMISSIONS   101

ESCROW ACCOUNT   153

ESTATE TAX   24, 33, 50-54, 66
    79, 110-114, 140, 220, 249

ESTATE PLAN
For Business   96
For Health Care   170

EXCLUDED RESOURCES 194-197

EXECUTOR   59

F

FAMILY
Partnership   108
Trust   130

FEDERAL RETIREE   236

FEE
Conservator   122, 173
Custodian   124
Guardian   174
Personal Repre. 20, 21, 59, 60
Trustee   46

FINANCIAL POWER OF ATTORNEY
     174-179, 247

FUNERAL, Preneed 153-157, 197

G

GENERAL
Partner   105-107
Power of Attorney   177

GIFT
Irrevocable   123
Prior   63
Specific   61, 66
Tax   51, 53, 54, 106
    110, 113, 145, 220
To Minor   122-126

201 Georgia Statutes and Regulations are referenced in
A Will Is Not Enough In Georgia

Each state has its own set of laws relating to the control, and protection of a person's Estate. The laws of Georgia relating to Guardianship, Probate and especially Medicaid are very different from the laws of other states.

The author is in the process of "translating" *A Will Is Not Enough* for the rest of the states; that is, writing state specific books that explain how to set up an Estate Plan for the given state and how to qualify for MEDICAID in that state.

A Will Is Not Enough is now available for:
ARIZONA, CALIFORNIA, CONNECTICUT, COLORADO
FLORIDA, HAWAII, INDIANA, ILLINOIS, MARYLAND
MICHIGAN, MASSACHUSETTS, NEBRASKA
NEW JERSEY, NEW MEXICO, NEW YORK,
OREGON, PENNSYLVANIA, TEXAS
VIRGINIA, WASHINGTON, WISCONSIN.

To check whether this book is currently available for other states call Eagle Publishing Company of Boca at
(800) 824-0823
or visit our Web site http://www.eaglepublishing.com

SPECIAL OFFER FOR PURCHASERS OF THIS BOOK
$25 INCLUDES SHIPPING

How To Defend Yourself Against Your Lawyer

is a book about the unhappy experiences people have with their lawyers, beginning with that of the author AMELIA E. POHL. She became involved in a law suit and found herself in the role of client, rather than lawyer. She become concerned about lawyers who do not provide their clients with the loyalty and respect due to them. This book is a result of those concerns.

The book is divided into chapters that cover the most common problems that take people to a lawyer: divorce, probate, criminal, personal injury, starting a business, making a Will, buying a house, etc. Each chapter tells of the misadventures of the unwary as they sought the services of a lawyer without a clue as to what they were "buying." This book is funny, sad, interesting, but most of all informative. It tells the reader how to become a savvy consumer, i.e., how to find the right lawyer for the right job. If the reader ever finds the need to employ a lawyer, he will be glad he read this book.

Copyright 2004   272 pages 6" X 9" soft cover
$20 includes Shipping and Handling

Beyond Grief To Acceptance and Peace

AMELIA E. POHL and the noted psychologist BARBARA J. SIMMONDS, Ph.d, have written a book for those families who have suffered a loss.

What to say to the bereaved
- ✧ How to help a child through the loss
- ✧ Strategies to adjust to a new life-style
- ✧ When and where to seek assistance.

80 pages   6" X 9" $10 includes Shipping and Handling

Guiding Those Left Behind

Amelia E. Pohl has written a series of books explaining how to settle an Estate. Each book is state specific, telling how things are done in that state. Each book explains:

✧ who to notify
✧ how to locate the decedent's property
✧ how to get possession of the inheritance
✧ when you do, and do not, need an attorney
✧ the rights of a beneficiary, and much more.

Each book is written with the assistance of an experienced attorney who is licensed and is practicing in that state.

The *Guiding* series is currently available for the following states: ALABAMA, ARIZONA, ARKANSAS, CALIFORNIA
CONNECTICUT, FLORIDA, GEORGIA, HAWAII, ILLINOIS
INDIANA, IOWA, KENTUCKY, LOUISIANA, MASSACHUSETTS
MARYLAND, MICHIGAN, MINNESOTA, MISSOURI
MISSISSIPPI, NEW JERSEY, NEW YORK
NORTH CAROLINA, OHIO, OKLAHOMA
PENNSYLVANIA, SOUTH CAROLINA, TENNESSEE
TEXAS, VIRGINIA, WASHINGTON, WISCONSIN

Visit our Web site http://www.eaglepublishing.com
to check whether books for other states are available at this time.

SPECIAL OFFER FOR PURCHASERS OF THIS BOOK
$24 INCLUDES SHIPPING

To order call (800) 824-0823

It is the goal of EAGLE PUBLISHING COMPANY to keep our publications fresh.

As we receive information about changes to the federal or BASE law we will post an update to this edition at our Web site:

http://www.eaglepublishing.com